823.
8
DIC
BLO

Charles Dickens.

WITHDRAWN

DATE			

CHARLES
DICKENS

COMPREHENSIVE RESEARCH
AND STUDY GUIDE

BLOOM'S
MAJOR
NOVELISTS

EDITED AND WITH AN
INTRODUCTION BY HAROLD BLOOM

CURRENTLY AVAILABLE

BLOOM'S MAJOR DRAMATISTS

Anton Chekhov
Henrik Ibsen
Arthur Miller
Eugene O'Neill
Shakespeare's Comedies
Shakespeare's Histories
Shakespeare's Romances
Shakespeare's Tragedies
George Bernard Shaw
Tennessee Williams

BLOOM'S MAJOR NOVELISTS

Jane Austen
The Brontës
Willa Cather
Charles Dickens
William Faulkner
F. Scott Fitzgerald
Nathaniel Hawthorne
Ernest Hemingway
Toni Morrison
John Steinbeck
Mark Twain
Alice Walker

BLOOM'S MAJOR SHORT STORY WRITERS

William Faulkner
F. Scott Fitzgerald
Ernest Hemingway
O. Henry
James Joyce
Herman Melville
Flannery O'Connor
Edgar Allan Poe
J. D. Salinger
John Steinbeck
Mark Twain
Eudora Welty

BLOOM'S MAJOR WORLD POETS

Geoffrey Chaucer
Emily Dickinson
John Donne
T. S. Eliot
Robert Frost
Langston Hughes
John Milton
Edgar Allan Poe
Shakespeare's Poems & Sonnets
Alfred, Lord Tennyson
Walt Whitman
William Wordsworth

BLOOM'S NOTES

The Adventures of Huckleberry Finn
Aeneid
The Age of Innocence
Animal Farm
The Autobiography of Malcolm X
The Awakening
Beloved
Beowulf
Billy Budd, Benito Cereno, & Bartleby the Scrivener
Brave New World
The Catcher in the Rye
Crime and Punishment
The Crucible

Death of a Salesman
A Farewell to Arms
Frankenstein
The Grapes of Wrath
Great Expectations
The Great Gatsby
Gulliver's Travels
Hamlet
Heart of Darkness & The Secret Sharer
Henry IV, Part One
I Know Why the Caged Bird Sings
Iliad
Inferno
Invisible Man
Jane Eyre
Julius Caesar

King Lear
Lord of the Flies
Macbeth
A Midsummer Night's Dream
Moby-Dick
Native Son
Nineteen Eighty-Four
Odyssey
Oedipus Plays
Of Mice and Men
The Old Man and the Sea
Othello
Paradise Lost
A Portrait of the Artist as a Young Man
The Portrait of a Lady

Pride and Prejudice
The Red Badge of Courage
Romeo and Juliet
The Scarlet Letter
Silas Marner
The Sound and the Fury
The Sun Also Rises
A Tale of Two Cities
Tess of the D'Urbervilles
Their Eyes Were Watching God
To Kill a Mockingbird
Uncle Tom's Cabin
Wuthering Heights

CHARLES
DICKENS

COMPREHENSIVE RESEARCH
AND STUDY GUIDE

BLOOM'S
MAJOR
NOVELISTS

EDITED AND WITH AN INTRODUCTION
BY HAROLD BLOOM

© 2000 by Chelsea House Publishers, a division of Main Line Book Co.

Introduction © 2000 by Harold Bloom

Printed and bound in the United States of America.

First Printing
1 3 5 7 9 8 6 4 2

Library of Congress Cataloging-in-Publication Data
Charles Dickens / edited by Harold Bloom
    120 p.   cm. — (Bloom's major novelists)
Includes bibliographical references (p. 112) and index
Summary: A comprehensive research and study guide for several novels
by Charles Dickens, including plot summaries, thematic analyses, lists
of characters, and critical views.
ISBN 0-7910-5251-6
1. Dickens, Charles, 1812–1870—Examinations—Study guides.
[1. Dickens, Charles, 1812–1870—Criticism and interpretation.   2. English
literature—History and criticism.]   I. Bloom, Harold.   II. Series.
PR4588.C358   1999
823'.8—dc21   99–29506
                                                           CIP

Chelsea House Publishers
1974 Sproul Road, Suite 400
Broomall, PA 19008-0914

The Chelsea House world wide web
address is www.chelseahouse.com

Contributing Editor: Tenley Williams

Contents

User's Guide

This volume is designed to present biographical, critical, and bibliographical information on the author's best-known or most important works. Following Harold Bloom's editor's note and introduction is a detailed biography of the author, discussing major life events and important literary accomplishments. A plot summary of each novel follows, tracing significant themes, patterns, and motifs in the work.

A selection of critical extracts, derived from previously published material from leading critics, analyzes aspects of each work. The extracts consist of statements from the author, if available, early reviews of the work, and later evaluations up to the present. A bibliography of the author's writings (including a complete list of all works written, cowritten, edited, and translated), a list of additional books and articles on the author and his or her work, and an index of themes and ideas in the author's writings conclude the volume.

~

Harold Bloom is Sterling Professor of the Humanities at Yale University and Henry W. and Albert A. Berg Professor of English at the New York University Graduate School. He is the author of over 20 books and the editor of more than 30 anthologies of literary criticism.

Professor Bloom's works include *Shelley's Mythmaking* (1959), *The Visionary Company* (1961), *Blake's Apocalypse* (1963), *Yeats* (1970), *A Map of Misreading* (1975), *Kabbalah and Criticism* (1975), and *Agon: Toward a Theory of Revisionism* (1982). *The Anxiety of Influence* (1973) sets forth Professor Bloom's provocative theory of the literary relationships between the great writers and their predecessors. His most recent books include *The American Religion* (1992), *The Western Canon* (1994), *Omens of Millennium: The Gnosis of Angels, Dreams, and Resurrection* (1996), and *Shakespeare: The Invention of the Human* (1998), a finalist for the 1998 National Book Award.

Professor Bloom earned his Ph.D. from Yale University in 1955 and has served on the Yale faculty since then. He is a 1985 MacArthur Foundation Award recipient, served as the Charles Eliot Norton Professor of Poetry at Harvard University in 1987–88, and has received honorary degrees from the universities of Rome and Bologna. In 1999, Professor Bloom received the prestigious American Academy of Arts and Letters Gold Medal for Criticism.

Currently, Harold Bloom is the editor of numerous Chelsea House volumes of literary criticism, including the series BLOOM'S NOTES, BLOOM'S MAJOR SHORT STORY WRITERS, BLOOM'S MAJOR POETS, MAJOR LITERARY CHARACTERS, MODERN CRITICAL VIEWS, MODERN CRITICAL INTERPRETATIONS, and WOMEN WRITERS OF ENGLISH AND THEIR WORKS.

Editor's Note

My Introduction centers upon *Great Expectations,* finding in it a wonderful balance between autobiographical closeness and aesthetic distancing.

The Critical Views, being more than two dozen, defy any simple summary. All of them are highly useful. I myself find particularly helpful H. M. Daleskie and A. E. Dyson on *Great Expectations;* J. Hillis Miller on *Bleak House;* Dickens himself and the poet Swinburne on *David Copperfield;* and John Gross and Edwin M. Eigner on *A Tale of Two Cities.*

Introduction

HAROLD BLOOM

Together with *David Copperfield, Great Expectations* is Dickens's most personal novel. He reread *Copperfield* "to be quite sure I had fallen into no unconscious repetitions" in composing *Great Expectations,* and his wariness helped make Pip his most complex protagonist. We hear Dickens's early traumas again in Pip's voice, and yet the author maintains considerable distance from Pip, as he scarcely does from David Copperfield, whose destiny is to become a Dickensian novelist.

Pip, like Copperfield, is a superb narrator, but he is frequently unkind to himself, and the reader is not expected to share in the severity of Pip's excessive self-condemnations, which partly ensue from his imaginative strength. Pip's imagination always mixes love and guilt, which is very much the mode of Charles Dickens.

George Bernard Shaw, introducing a reprint of *Great Expectations,* remarked that "Pip, like his creator, has no culture and no religion." We need to recall that Shaw told us also that he felt only pity for an even greater writer, whenever he compared the mind of Shakespeare with his own! Shaw's religion was a peculiar kind of Creative Evolution, and his culture compares poorly with his contemporary Oscar Wilde's. Dickens indeed was a Dickensian in religion, and was deeply grounded in popular culture, as well as in literary culture.

Whether Pip's obsessive and unmerited guilt owes more to popular traditions of shame-culture, or emanates from literary guilt-culture, is very difficult to determine. One critic, Shuli Barzilai, wisely conjectures that Pip's guilt has a deep source in what Freud called "family romances," so that his relationship with Estella is quasi-incestuous, she being (unknowingly) Magwitch's daughter, while Pip becomes the escaped convict's adopted son. What is clear enough is that both Pip and Estella seem doomed to expiate a guilt not at all their own, the guilt of the fathers and the mothers.

Dickens notoriously weakened *Great Expectations* by revising its ending, so that Pip and Estella might be viewed as living together happily ever after. This revision is manifestly at variance with the imaginative spirit of the novel, and is best ignored. Pip, properly read, remains a permanent emblem of something that Dickens could not forgive in himself. ❀

Biography of
Charles Dickens

Charles John Huffam Dickens was born in Landport, Portsea, near Portsmouth, England, on February 7, 1812, the second of eight children of John and Elizabeth Barrow Dickens. The family moved to London in 1814, to Chatham in 1817, and then back to London in 1822. By 1824 increasing financial difficulties caused Dickens's father to be briefly imprisoned for debt; Dickens himself was put to work for a few months at a shoe-blacking warehouse. Memories of this painful period in his life were to influence much of his later writing, in particular the early chapters of *David Copperfield*.

After studying at the Wellington House Academy in London (1824–27), Dickens worked as a solicitor's clerk (1827–28), then worked for various newspapers, first the *True Sun* (1832–34) and later as a political reporter for the *Morning Chronicle* (1834–36). In 1833 Dickens fell in love with Maria Beadnell, but her family opposed any contemplated marriage. Dickens never forgot Maria, and she served as the model for Dora in *David Copperfield*.

In 1836 a collection of articles contributed to various periodicals appeared in two volumes as *Sketches by "Boz," Illustrative of Every-day Life and Every-day People.* This was followed by the enormously popular *Posthumous Papers of the Pickwick Club* (1836–37). Like many of Dickens's later novels, the *Pickwick Papers* first appeared in a series of monthly chapbooks or "parts." Other novels were serialized in magazines before appearing in book form. In 1836 Dickens married Catherine Hogarth, with whom he had ten children before their separation in 1858. At the beginning of his marriage, Catherine's sixteen-year-old sister Mary lived with them, but she died after a few months. The shock of this loss affected Dickens permanently, and Mary would be the model for many of the pure, saintly heroines in his novels—such as Little Nell in *The Old Curiosity Shop*—who die at an early age.

Between 1837 and 1839 Dickens published a second novel, *Oliver Twist*, in monthly installments in *Bentley's Miscellany*, a new periodical of which he was the first editor. This was followed in 1838–39 by *Nicholas Nickleby*. Dickens then founded his own weekly, *Master Humphrey's Clock* (1840–41), in which appeared his novels *The Old Curiosity Shop* and *Barnaby Rudge*. In 1842 he and his wife visited the United States and Canada, and after returning Dickens published *American Notes* (1842), two volumes of impressions that caused much offense in the United States. He then wrote *Martin Chuzzlewit* (1843–44), a novel set partly in America.

In 1843 Dickens published *A Christmas Carol*, the first in a series of Christmas books that included *The Chimes* (1845), *The Cricket on the Hearth* (1846), *The Battle of Life* (1846), and *The Haunted Man and the Ghost's Bargain* (1848). Early in 1846 he was for a brief time the editor of the *Daily News*, a paper of the Radical party to which he contributed "Pictures of Italy" after visiting Italy in 1844 and again in 1845. During a visit to Switzerland in 1846 Dickens wrote his novel *Dombey and Son*, which appeared monthly between 1846 and 1848. In 1850 he started the periodical *Household Words;* in 1859 it was incorporated into *All the Year Round*, which Dickens continued to edit until his death. Much of his later work was published in these two periodicals, including *David Copperfield* (1849–50), *Bleak House* (1852–53), *Hard Times* (1854), *Little Dorrit* (1855–57), *A Tale of Two Cities* (1859), *Great Expectations* (1860–61), and *Our Mutual Friend* (1864–65).

Throughout his life, Dickens threw himself vigorously into a variety of social and political crusades, such as prison reform, improvement of education, the status of workhouses, and reform of the copyright law (American publishers were notorious for pirating his works and offering him no compensation). These interests find their way also into his work, which is characterized by sympathy for the oppressed and a keen examination of class distinctions. His novels and stories have been both praised and censured for their sentimentality and their depiction of "larger-than-life" characters, such as Pickwick or Mr. Micawber (in *David Copperfield*).

During the last twenty years of his life Dickens still found time to direct amateur theatrical productions, sometimes of his own plays. He also became involved in a variety of philanthropical activities, gave public readings, and in 1867–68 visited America for a second time. Dickens died suddenly on June 9, 1870, leaving unfinished his last novel, *The Mystery of Edwin Drood*, which was first published later that same year. Several editions of his collected letters have been published. Despite his tremendous popularity during and after his own life, it was not until the twentieth century that serious critical study of his work began to appear. Modern critical opinion has tended to favor the later, more somber and complex works over the earlier ones characterized by boisterous humor and broad caricature. ❀

Plot Summary of
Great Expectations

Great Expectations is in many ways typical of Charles Dickens's numerous novels. It is narrated in an exuberant and verbally playful style. It teems with a wide variety of odd, obsessive, wonderfully vivid characters. In mood, it runs the full range from hilarity to sentimental tenderness to merciless satire to gothic melodrama and violence to crime-fiction suspense. It describes village, town, and city life. It portrays the upper, middle, and lower classes, including the criminal underworld. It probes the deepest loves and fears, hopes and disappointments of a maturing boy. And it offers a dark vision of the psychological effects of the particular kind of class-society fostered by industrial capitalism in nineteenth-century England. Yet *Great Expectations* is atypical of Dickens's work in that it manages to contain all this within a relatively economical plot. Unlike many of Dickens's more diffuse, open-ended narratives, *Great Expectations* is carefully organized so that at each new turn of events the main character and narrator, Philip Pirrip (Pip), learns more about himself by learning more about the complex social web in which he is enmeshed.

We first meet Pip on the day before Christmas, near the small cottage where he lives with his shrewish and abusive older sister, "Mrs. Joe," and her husband Joe Gargery, a kindly blacksmith (**chapter one**). His moral education begins when, as he sits by the graves of his parents and five siblings, he is roughly seized by a convict still wearing a chain around his leg. The man holds Pip upside down and shakes him until his pockets are emptied. He threatens to tear Pip's heart and liver out unless he promises to get him food. Pip returns with food and the man thanks him; he then sets out in pursuit of another convict, one Pip had already spotted on the marshes. In **chapter two** Pip realizes that the food he gave away had been intended for the holiday dinner. As Pip bolts for the door to escape his sister's wrath, soldiers arrive asking Joe to help capture an escaped convict. Pip must accompany Joe and he fears that the convict will think Pip has brought the soldiers. When the convict is caught, however, he covers for Pip, telling Joe that he himself had stolen the food from the house. "Poor, miserable, fellow creature," Joe says, with typical compassion. In **chapter seven** Pip, as the adult narrator, reflects upon the contrast between Joe's trusting kindness and his own cunning and "cowardly" acts. But his awareness of his weakness does not allow him to overcome it. His continual disloyalties to Joe, by lies and thefts, form the most painful part of Pip's moral education.

The next phase of this education begins in **chapter eight** when Pip receives a communication from Miss Havisham, "an immensely rich and grim lady who lived in a large and dismal house barricaded against robbers, and who led a life of seclusion." She wants Pip to ease her loneliness by playing at her house. Mrs. Joe hopes that the old woman will "do something" to advance Pip in society and sends him off, promptly.

Miss Havisham explains to Pip that she has not seen daylight since before he was born, and he later finds out that she has neither changed her clothes, nor wound the clocks, nor altered any detail since the wedding day many years ago when the groom jilted her. Her only interest is to train Estella, the young girl who lives with her, to take revenge upon all males. Estella viciously mocks Pip for his uncouth language, his "coarse" hands, and his "thick" boots.

The shame and self-hatred that Pip "catches" from Estella lie at the dark psychological core of Dickens's novel. Above all else, *Great Expectations* is a book about social class; about how in a class-based society like that of Victorian England class discriminations seep into and contaminate the deepest and subtlest levels of human feeling and motivation. From the moment that Estella disdains Pip as a "common laboring boy," Pip's feelings and attitudes toward things are fundamentally altered. He begins to have new ambitions for book learning and correct speech. He becomes self-conscious about clothing and appearances. He begins to feel ambivalent about the prospect of following a career as a blacksmith. He becomes critical of the rough casualness of his rural surroundings. And most damaging, he loses the capacity for spontaneous uncritical intimacy with his closest companion, Joe. Pip's attitudes come to be shaped by the class divisions which structure his society as a whole. To reveal this painful process to the eyes of his readers was perhaps Dickens's principal thematic aim in *Great Expectations*.

Pip decides that he will become "a gentleman." But his aspirations are checked when Miss Havisham purchases his "indentures," thereby making him legally an apprentice to Joe (**chapter eleven**).

For Joe and the people in the village the securing of the apprentice-ship is a cause for celebration, but for Pip it is only a sad reminder of the distance between his world and that of Estella. Because of Joe, the narrator reflects, he had once held the profession of blacksmith sacred, but now it seems "coarse and common." Over the next four years the hope the Miss Havisham will someday make his fortune sustains him—until she tells him that Estella has been sent to Europe to be trained "for a lady," and that she herself will have nothing more to do with him.

Upon returning from town one day (**chapter fifteen**) Pip dis-covers that Mrs. Joe has been nearly killed by a tremendous blow to the head. The only evidence on the scene is a convict's leg-irons. Pip feels immediately guilty that he may have contributed to the crime by helping to liberate the perpetrator. The mystery remains unsolved, and is soon forgotten, when, in **chapter eighteen**, a "bul-lying man" named Jaggers tells Pip that he has "great expectations"; that he has "come into a handsome property," and that he will be brought up a gentleman. All this on the condition that Joe release Pip from his "indentures," that his benefactor remain a secret, and that Pip agree always to be called Pip. Surprisingly, Joe agrees. Her-bert Pocket will be Pip's tutor and Jaggers will be his guardian. Pip buys new clothes and goes to London.

Pip's good fortune immediately goes to his head (**chapter nine-teen**). As he leaves the village, he looks with condescension on everyone in the village, eager to leave them all behind. His passage from the country to the city is significant both as decisive stage in his own personal history, and as a marker of an important feature of the sociological landscape of Victorian England. In moving away from the village world Pip leaves behind a stable, deeply rooted, tradi-tional community where everyone was known and where the home and the workplace were often close by and integrated. Arriving in London, he encounters an anonymous, quickly changing, unfamiliar world of transients and hard-nosed professionals for whom work life and home life are sharply separated. Where physical strength, manual know-how, and the familiar were valued in the village, abstract knowledge, professional prestige, and money are valued in the city. This contrast in value-systems is rendered most vividly in Pip's encounters with the lawyer Mr. Jaggers and his assistant, Mr. Wemmick (**chapter twenty**).

In **chapters twenty-four** through **thirty-four** Pip spends much of his time indulging in a period of callow and irresponsible adolescence. A generous allowance allows him to run up large debts. He courts Estella slavishly when she returns from Europe, but is out—outclassed, as it were—by another suitor. On the one occasion that Joe visits him in London (**chapter twenty-seven**), he is hopelessly self-conscious and out of place at Pip's sophisticated table, and Pip finds himself irritated and embarrassed. Joe leaves quickly, but in one of the novel's saddest moments, he remarks upon the disruption of their former intimacy: "You and me is not two figures to be together in London; nor yet anywhere else but what is private, and known, and understood among friends."

Soon after, in **chapter thirty-five**, Pip returns to the forge on the occasion of Mrs. Joe's death. He is jostled by conflicting emotions of guilt and relief as he confronts mortality close up for the first time. As he leaves, Pip is pained to see Joe attempt to wipe the coal from his hand before he shakes hands with his now genteel former companion.

In **chapter thirty-nine** Pip discovers that his benefactor is none other than the convict he had encountered in the marsh long ago: Abel Magwitch returned from banishment to Australia a rich man. His sole purpose in achieving this success had been to make a gentleman out of the little blacksmith's boy who had once come to this aid. All Pip's illusions are now dashed. Estella is surely not designed for him and, most painful of all, he now knows that he abandoned Joe not for a higher social station, but for an alliance with a criminal. A shock equal to this one comes in **chapters fifty** and **fifty-one**, when Pip ascertains that Magwitch is Estella's father!

Among the concluding sequences of the novel (**chapters fifty-two** through **fifty-nine**) Pip passes into a delirious exhausted illness for several days. He awakens in the gentle care of Joe, who has paid his debts. He has one last encounter with Estella, who tells him of the unhappiness of her life and the failure of her marriage. In the original version of the novel their meeting is merely warm and cordial, and Pip sees that Estella's difficult experiences have made her wiser. In a revised version, Dickens implies that they are permanently reunited. ❀

List of Characters in
Great Expectations

Pip (**Philip Pirrip**) is the hero and narrating voice of *Great Expectations*. An orphan left in the care of a shrewish older sister and her blacksmith husband, he aspires to become a gentleman in order to win the heart of a haughty girl, Estella, with whom he falls in love. Money from an anonymous benefactor allows him to move away from the rural village in which he grew up to the city of London, where he sets himself up as a gentleman. Surprising turns of events and unexpected connections between the people he meets teach him about the nature of his society and about the permanent value of his childhood loyalties.

Joe Gargery is, as Pip describes him, "a mild, good-natured, sweet-tempered, easy-going, foolish, dear fellow—a sort of Hercules in strength, and also in weakness." A blacksmith, he is married to Pip's older sister, and is both Pip's guardian and close companion early in the novel. He and Pip enjoy a variety of droll "larks," and Joe attempts to shield Pip from abusive treatment by his older sister. Pip's genteel aspirations and affectations later strain their intimacy, but Joe remains loyal to Pip, and comes to his aid when he finds him in trouble. Joe embodies the virtues of the English working class as Dickens understood them, and stands at the sentimental heart of the novel.

Mrs. Joe is Pip's older sister and surrogate mother. Resentful that she must raise Pip "by hand" and that her husband is merely a blacksmith, she physically and verbally abuses both of them. She eventually dies as a result of a hammer blow to her head. The identity of her assailant is one of several mysteries which drive the plot.

Biddy, a wise and kindly relative of Mr. Wopsle, helps to educate Pip and becomes his confidante. She teaches him reading and writing, as well as some important lessons in basic human decency. After Mrs. Joe's death, she marries Joe, and they have a child who is named after Pip.

Abel Magwitch (**Provis**) is an escaped convict who is also Pip's anonymous benefactor, Estella's unknown father, one of Jaggers's clients, and the former lover of Jaggers's maid Molly. Pip snitches food and a file for him at the beginning of the novel, thus earning his lifelong gratitude and support. From his exile in Australia, he secretly sends the money which enables Pip to educate himself and to become a gentleman. He is captured and dies in prison after returning to England toward the end of the novel.

Miss Havisham is an extremely wealthy and eccentric old lady who has secluded herself in her house for twenty years, since the day her would-be husband failed to show up for their wedding. She still dresses in her wedding outfit, refuses to move anything from the place it occupied on her wedding day, and has stopped all the clocks. Her only interest in life is to train her young charge, Estella, to take revenge on the male sex. Pip finally makes her see that she has deprived Estella of her humanity, and she begs Pip's forgiveness and immolates herself out of remorse.

Estella is a very pretty, haughty, and cold-hearted girl with whom Pip falls hopelessly in love upon first seeing her at Miss Havisham's house. She is raised by Miss Havisham to take revenge on all men, and she performs this role effectively in her treatment of Pip. She eventually marries a wealthy lout for his money, and suffers an unhappy marriage and a separation. Unbeknownst to her she is the daughter of the convict Magwitch and Jaggers's maid, Molly.

Herbert Pocket, upon first meeting Pip in the courtyard of Miss Havisham's house, says to him, "Let's fight." Pip proceeds to knock him down several times, but when they meet again years later in London they become the closest of friends. They take rooms together, and Herbert draws tactfully on his genteel upbringing to help Pip smooth out some of his rough edges. Pip uses his fortune to help Herbert get started in business, and eventually goes to work in the same firm. At the close of the novel we are told that Pip goes to live with Herbert and his wife.

Jaggers is a brilliant and domineering lawyer who provides the link between the various social levels depicted in the novel. He administers the financial affairs of both Miss Havisham and Magwitch, and becomes Pip's legal sponsor. He functions as a symbol of urban professionalism at its best and worst extremes. He is efficient, punctual, articulate, and dynamic; but he is also impersonal, cold, arrogant, and obsessed with control.

Wemmick is Jaggers's assistant. Like Jaggers, Wemmick is grimly professional in his capacity as an agent of the law. His motto is "get sortable property" (i.e., money). But Pip finds that behind the walls of a home that is literally his castle, he is spontaneous, kind, and playful. He takes tender care of his aging father, and goes to great lengths to help Pip and Herbert Pocket.

Bentley Drummle is an aristocratic rival of Pip's for the attentions of Estella. He is described as unintelligent, selfish, deceitful, and proud. His family riches nonetheless win him Estella's hand in marriage.

Orlick is a violent, resentful, and dangerous journeyman blacksmith. He bludgeons Mrs. Joe with a hammer early in the novel, and in the closing moments he very nearly kills Pip.

Pumblechook is an alternately pompous and obsequious corn-chandler who is a friend of Mrs. Joe. He lectures Pip about the natural viciousness of children until Pip comes into money, at which point he fawns upon him shamelessly.

Compeyson is the second convict Pip sees on the marshes at the beginning of the novel. His sophisticated upbringing allowed him to take terrible advantage of Magwitch when they were partners in crime, and Magwitch is thus determined to take revenge upon him at all costs. He is also the man who left Miss Havisham standing at the altar, and made off with a good deal of her money. ❊

Critical Views on
Great Expectations

SYLVÈRE MONOD ON THE MORALITY OF
GREAT EXPECTATIONS

[Sylvère Monod, a former professor of English at the Sorbonne in Paris, is a leading scholar on Dickens. He has written *Dickens the Novelist* (1968) and a study, *Martin Chuzzlewit* (1985), and (with George Lord) has edited *Hard Times* (1966) and *Bleak House* (1977). In this extract, Monod finds the true significance of *Great Expectations* to lie in its moral outlook, particularly in its scorn of snobbery and the worship of money.]

⟨M⟩uch of the significance of *Great Expectations* to-day comes from the moral and social purport of the book. Here again, the extraordinary wealth of its implications and suggestions in those fields, will be best appreciated by each individual reader when he has discovered them for himself, when they have thus become part of his moral experience; and the force of those revelations and confirmations will be increased after each fresh contact with the book. I for one am warned by repeated past experience—and by experience in the very recent past—against regarding any of my own findings as final, or the list as closed. Besides, such discoveries are intensely personal matters, so that they can hardly be shared, least of all publicly. And the different findings of different readers need not be mutually exclusive; the moral truth in *Great Expectations* is manifold, and can be apprehended in any number of fragmentary ways. I can do no more therefore, than mention one of the most significant directions in which I at present think this truth is to be looked for. I tend to see in *Great Expectations,* in so far as social and moral criticism is at stake, above all a passionate denunciation of the false values on which the Victorian ideals of gentlemanliness rested: humbug—that lifelong bugbear of Dickens—smugness, and all the snobberies entailed by an exclusive regard for, or even worship of, money and its consequences in the form of rank, are all tirelessly and relentlessly exposed.

Now, this, if it were all, even expressed with exceptional vigour, the vigour of strong personal conviction, would be most unoriginal, and it would not justify the claim I am trying to make. Perhaps both Carlyle and Ruskin, among others, were preaching the same creed with greater moral elevation and greater efficacy. But I think this is not all. For indeed, thanks to the autobiographical form, Dickens can picture the groping quest of Pip for the truth, not only about the world and the society among which he lives, but also, and more importantly, about himself. Thus he will perceive his own deficiencies, and such perceptions will be as many steps in his spiritual progress. Sometimes he will not be aware of them, but will disclose them to us unwillingly, as it were, or at any rate unwittingly, and they will be all the more significant to us on that account.

Thus does Dickens make it abundantly clear that the worst and most insidious kind of smugness may lie in the complacent, Pharisaical, condemnation of other people's smugness. Pip, even while he lays bare the humbug of Pumblechook, or the sycophantic greed of Miss Havisham's relatives, or the snobbery of his comrade Drummle, is a pitiful little snob himself. The word *snob* is not used once by Dickens in *Great Expectations,* yet a considerable proportion of the book consists of infinite and subtle variations on this theme of snobbery. One thing is rather explicitly brought to light; it is that Pip will never be a man before he has ceased to wish to become merely a gentleman, before he has discarded all his spurious ambitions. This is already of the utmost significance, and it is beautifully conveyed. But I think the implications of Pip's moral adventure are much more far-reaching than that. And what makes the book so exceedingly valuable even to-day, a hundred years after, is perhaps above all the effect it must inevitably produce on us, the suggestion that it will never do to lay the whole blame on the Victorians; such a comfortable attitude would be a hindrance, not a help, on the way to truth and moral progress. *Great Expectations* invites us to turn our ruthless glance on to ourselves, and to see that there is smugness, that there is humbug, that there is Victorianism of a kind, that there is this yearning for pseudo-gentility and this unslakable thirst for money, not in the Victorians merely, but in man in general, in the men of all times, in the men of the present day, in us.

And then, in the same way as Pip emerges out of his ordeal with clearer perceptions, we can emerge out of the reading and re-reading of *Great Expectations* with a better understanding of some vital truths. *Great Expectations* is probably Dickens's most fully adult novel, staging as it does in Pip an adult in the making; why not let the book help make adults of all its readers? Then would the title of the novel, unquestionably far and away the richest, most beautiful, most pathetic of the whole fifteen coined by Dickens, assume an ever fresh significance. Pip's expectations were as deceptive as they were, not great, but contemptibly little; so were Miss Havisham's, or Magwitch's. But our own expectations on opening the book, for the first or the hundredth time, cannot be disappointed, whether we go to it for amusement, or for emotion, or for what alone can make expectations truly great: the truth.

—Sylvère Monod, "Great Expectations a Hundred Years After," *Dickensian* 56 (1960): pp. 139–140.

☙

JULIAN MOYNAHAN ON PIP AS DICKENS'S MOST COMPLEX HERO

[Julian Moynahan, a professor of English at Rutgers University, is a novelist and critic. He has written *Vladimir Nabokov* (1971), *Anglo-Irish: The Literary Imagination in a Hyphenated Culture* (1995), and other works. In this extract, Moynahan finds Pip to be Dickens's most complex hero in his combination of virtues and flaws.]

In this essay I have argued that Dickens's novel defines its hero's dream of great expectations and the consequences stemming from indulgence in that dream under the two aspects of desire and will, of regressive longing for an excess of love and of violent aggressiveness. In the unfolding of the action these two dramas are not presented separately. Instead they are combined into Dickens's most complex representation of character in action. Pip is Dickens's most complicated hero, demonstrating at once the traits of criminal and gull, of victimiser and victim. He is victimised by his dream and the dream itself, by virtue of its profoundly anti-social and unethical nature, forces him into relation with a world in which other human beings fall victim to his drive for power. He is, in short, a hero sinned against and sinning: sinned against because in the first place the dream was thrust upon the helpless child by powerful and corrupt figures from the adult world; a sinner because in accepting for himself a goal in life based upon unbridled individualism and indifference to others he takes up a career which *Great Expectations* repeatedly, through a variety of artistic means, portrays as essentially criminal.

After Magwitch's death, Pip falls a prey to brain fever. During his weeks of delirium it seems to me that his hallucinations articulate the division in his character between helpless passivity and demonic aggressiveness. Pip tells us he dreamed

> that I was a brick in the house wall, and yet entreating to be released from the giddy place where the builders had set me; that I was a steel beam of a vast engine clashing and whirling over a great gulf, yet that I implored in my own person to have the engine stopped, and my part in it hammered off.

It is tempting to read these images as dream logic. The hero-victim cries for release from his unsought position of height and power, but cannot help himself from functioning as a moving part of a monstrous apparatus which seems to sustain itself from a plunge into the abyss only through the continuous expenditure of destructive force. In the narrative's full context this vast engine can be taken to represent at one and the same time the demonic side of the hero's career and a society that maintains its power intact by the continuous destruction of the hopes and lives of its weaker members. In the latter connection we can think of Magwitch's account of his childhood and youth, and of the judge who passed a death sentence on thirty-two men and women, while the sun struck in through the courtroom windows making a 'broad shaft of light between the two-and-thirty and the judge, linking them both together'. But to think of the engine as a symbol of society is still to think of Pip. For Pip's career enacts his society's condition of being—its guilt, its sinfulness, and in the end, its helplessness to cleanse itself of a taint 'of prison and crime'.

When Pip wakes up from his delirium he finds himself a child again, safe in the arms of the angelic Joe Gargery. But the guilt of great expectations remains inexpiable, and the cruelly beautiful original ending of the novel remains the only possible 'true' ending. Estella and Pip face each other across the insurmountable barrier of lost innocence. The novel dramatises the loss of innocence, and does not glibly present the hope of a redemptory second birth for either its guilty hero or the guilty society which shaped him. I have already said that Pip's fantasy of superabundant love brings him at last to a point of alienation from the real world. And similarly Pip's fantasy of power brings him finally to a point where withdrawal is the only positive moral response left to him.

The brick is taken down from its giddy place, a part of the engine is hammered off. Pip cannot redeem his world. In no conceivable sense a leader, he can only lead himself into a sort of exile from his society's power centres. Living abroad as the partner of a small, unambitious firm, he is to devote his remaining life to doing the least possible harm to the smallest number of people, so earning a visitor's privileges in the lost paradise where Biddy and Joe, the genuine innocents of the novel, flourish in thoughtless content.

—Julian Moynahan, "The Hero's Guilt: The Case of *Great Expectations*," *Essays in Criticism* 10, no. 1 (January 1960): pp. 77–79.

HARRY STONE ON FAIRY-TALE ASPECTS OF *GREAT EXPECTATIONS*

[Harry Stone has written several books on Dickens, including *Dickens and the Invisible World* (1979) and *The Night Side of Dickens* (1994). In this extract, Stone finds that *Great Expectations* incorporates many aspects of the fairy tale, something Stone believes to be common throughout Dickens's work.]

The magical names of *Great Expectations* and the relationships they mirror or disguise are organic portions of the novel's fairy-tale conception. That conception controls the book again and again. Thus, though Pip fails to marry the true princess in the primary fairy tale, Joe, the true prince, does win her, and so fulfills a minor fairy tale theme. And though Pip's accrual of money proves a curse, Herbert's identical accrual of money (the fairy tale within the fairy tale) proves a blessing—and this not only to Herbert but to Pip. Pip's anonymous endowment of Herbert is the only good that comes of his expectations. By having the identical fairy-tale money given in the identical fairy-tale manner corrupt in one instance and save in the other, Dickens is showing that it is not money itself which corrupts but its improper use—a lesson elaborated by the money-giving of Magwitch and Miss Havisham. All this is so unobtrusively embedded in the action that it comes as something of a shock to discover that the rewards and retributions in *Great Expectations* are as carefully weighted as in the early novels. But now the rewards elaborate and fulfill the theme; in the early novels they wrenched it.

The fairy-tale configurations outlined here are buttressed by hundreds of complementary details. The onset and development of the magical relationship between Magwitch and Pip, for example, gains much from its fairy-tale associations. When Pip meets Magwitch he falls under his spell, a submission accompanied by ritualistic portents. The moment of yielding occurs at the instant Magwitch upends Pip—Magwitch's hypnotic eyes bore "powerfully down" into Pip's, while Pip's innocent eyes look "most helplessly" up into the convict's. In this fateful instant of weakness, Pip yields himself to evil, a yielding marked by a fairy-tale meeting of eyes, the first of many similar looks. Pip's dawning moment of individual identity is also a moment of taint and guilt. His subsequent sense of sinfulness is a realistic reflection of his contamination (a contamination which is really a part of the human condition, which is coeval with individuality and self-consciousness), but his contamination, like his induction, is also underlined by fairy-tale signs. The evil adult world impinges upon Pip in the same way that Dickens, in his own childhood, visualized a sadistic adult world impinging upon himself. The supreme imagery of evil is adapted from the imagery of fairy tales: it involves fateful glances, solemn compacts, ogres, cannibalism, and the like; and in each world the crucial relationship is the same: it centers about a brutal adult and a waiflike child. Yet the effect of the book is neither fabulous nor self-pitying. Dickens avoids the former distortion because his basic situation is psychologically realistic—it emerges from his own experiences; he avoids the latter because, although he surrounds Pip with an expressionistic reflection of his own childhood terror, he distances that terror through retrospective humor. For the reader, therefore, Pip's real but fairy-tale nightmare partakes of fairy-tale whimsey—a combination which allows Dickens to reveal and conceal his involvement.

Magwitch, for instance, threatens to eat Pip's "fat cheeks"—a threat that Pip accepts as literal. Later Magwitch swears to have Pip's heart and liver "tore out, roasted and ate," and he tells the trembling child of a bloodthirsty cohort who can "softly creep and creep his way to him and tear him open"—the exact threat Good Mrs. Brown terrified Florence with in *Dombey and Son*. This ogreish bullying is grotesque and amusing—for Dickens as well as the reader. But for Dickens it also carries a burden of undiminished horror, a burden made explicit by Pip's reactions and their consequences. Pip finds Magwitch's ferocious threats as real and endlessly ramifying as the young Dickens found the atrocities in "Captain Murderer" or "Chips and the Devil"—two blood-thirsty cannibalistic stories that he heard nightly from his nurse. (A key word in the terrorizing refrain of "Chips and the Devil" is "Pips.") As a result of Magwitch's cannibalistic threats, Pip enters into an indissoluble compact to aid him, and Pip's last glimpse of the outlaw occurs as he glances "over his shoulder" while racing homeward toward the forge. In that backward glance (so reminiscent of fateful glances in mythology and fairy lore) Pip sees Magwitch plunging toward the river, the flowing stream which runs symbolically through all of *Great Expectations* and which will ultimately convey Magwitch and himself to death and salvation.

—Harry Stone, "Fire, Hand, and Gate: Dickens' *Great Expectations*," *Kenyon Review* 24, no. 4 (Autumn 1962): pp. 678–680.

⊗

H. M. DALESKI ON THE USE OF THE FIRST PERSON IN *GREAT EXPECTATIONS*

[H. M. Daleski is the author of many critical studies, including *The Forked Flame: A Study of D. H. Lawrence* (1965), *The Divided Heroine* (1984), and *Unities: Studies in the English Novel* (1985). In this extract, taken from his book on Dickens, Daleski examines Dickens's choice of first-person narration in *Great Expectations,* which seems to have caused Dickens to unearth many autobiographical details in the portrayal of Pip.]

Great Expectations is one of Dickens's most personal novels, as personal, perhaps, even as *David Copperfield;* and consequently it bears the marks of his own cravings to an unusual degree. It has generally been held that Pip's passion for Estella, the most strongly expressed passion in the novels to this point, is a reflection of Dickens's feelings for Ellen Ternan; we may add that his relationship with the young actress is furthermore reflected in the emphasis in the novel on hidden relationship. But I would suggest that it was Dickens's decision to use Pip as a first-person narrator that determined the emotional centre of the novel, which is not the relationship of Pip and Estella. For Dickens this decision meant that his new novel would inevitably challenge comparison with *David Copperfield,* the only other work from which he had debarred himself as omniscient author; and to ensure that he did not repeat himself, he read the earlier novel again some six weeks before the first instalment of the new novel appeared: 'To be quite sure I had fallen into no unconscious repetitions, I read *David Copperfield* again the other day, and was affected by it to a degree you would hardly believe.' It seems at least likely that the use of the first-person method and the reading of *David Copperfield* reactivated Dickens's sense of his early traumatic experiences, particularly the sense of being abandoned by both his parents when he was sent to work at the blacking warehouse; and in the incalculable ways of the imagination this led to his unconsciously shaping the plot he had devised into a vehicle for the vicarious satisfaction of his own deepest need as a child. Certainly the matrix of the plot is the abandonment and rejection of children: Pip, the orphan, who has never seen his father and mother and is brought up by hand, has the continued sense as a child of being always treated as if he 'had insisted on being born in opposition to the dictates of reason, religion, and morality, and against the dissuading arguments of [his] best friends'; this is how Magwitch recounts his earliest memory: 'I first become aware of myself, down in Essex, a thieving turnips for my living. Summun had run away from me—a man—a tinker—and he'd took the fire with him, and left me wery cold'; and Estella, as a child, is handed over to Jaggers by her mother, to be done with as he sees fit. We may add that Miss

Havisham, though not a child, is abandoned by her lover on her wedding day.

—H. M. Daleski, *Dickens and the Art of Analogy* (New York: Schocken Books, 1970): pp. 241–242.

A. E. DYSON ON MAGWITCH

[A. E. Dyson is a distinguished British critic and author of *The Crazy Fabric: Essays in Irony* (1965) and, with Julian Lovelock, *Masterful Images: English Poetry from Metaphysicals to Romantics* (1976). He is a former Senior Lecturer in English and American Studies at the University of East Anglia. In this extract, Dyson focuses on the character of Magwitch, whom he believes to be a fundamentally decent individual in spite of his life as a criminal.]

In this devious plot, what if anything can be said for Magwitch, who so disastrously usurps Joe's place as second father to Pip? The small Pip had confided to him the loss of his father—indeed, Pip was attacked on his father's tombstone—so Magwitch at least knows, or thinks he knows, Pip's parental void. Further, he persuades himself that his undertaking is wholly unselfish; he chooses for his adopted son not some new name, as Betsey Trotwood had done for David, but the name 'Pip' that the child had given to himself. Here is an almost humble sense of Pip's identity, which Magwitch will respect, consciously at least, at every turn. There is the further sense that in giving Pip money and status he is rescuing him from his own former predicament, and giving the boy a unique chance of freedom and happiness in life. It must be admitted also that, misreading the young Pip's fear as pity, Magwitch has at least responded to pity with love instead of hate. His project compares not unfavourably with Miss Havisham's plans for Estella. Both adopt a child, and offer education, the one for making a lady, the other a gentleman, after the way of the world. Both are genuinely concerned for the child—in her way Miss Havisham loves Estella—and both use the child in a personal and delusional dream of revenge. But whereas Miss Havisham's 'revenge' is born of hatred, Magwitch's comes from a comparatively innocent pride. Estella is to provide for Miss Havisham the spectacle of males in agony; Pip is merely to charm himself, and society, and so to justify Magwitch's ruined life. The consciousness of for once in his life doing good sustains Magwitch, and helped along with oaths sworn on his pocket Bible, he achieves that most unusual thing in Dickens's novels or, indeed, in life as we know it, a genuine conversion from criminality in his middle age.

At root, it seems, Magwitch has always been decent; and it is part of Dickens's greatness to demonstrate just the psychological spur required to change him to the extent that we see. Yet it hardly needs adding that Magwitch's plan, in the aspects hidden from him, is a terrible violation of Pip, and at exactly that precious point—Pip's identity—which Magwitch thinks he respects. Pip is used as a thing in Magwitch's own strange fight for salvation, and from any perspective outside Magwitch the terrible consequences cry aloud to be seen. But it is of a piece with the delusional mentality that Magwitch cannot see from any other angle; and, moreover, that despite the stringent condition of secrecy laid upon Pip about his benefactor, he is privately convinced that Pip 'must know'. If it is so central to Magwitch's life, how can it be less so to Pip's? The boy will naturally and joyfully have detected his second father from the first.

Dickens nowhere makes these implications explicit, but embodies them in vividly brilliant scenes. They are unmistakeable in Magwitch's manner of revealing himself, and in the tone of affectionate ownership and complicity, unbearable to Pip, which he instinctively adopts. The lesson of Pip's snobbery to Joe, real and painful enough in such a horrible denouement, is one aspect only of a confrontation which Pip's reason barely survives. Little wonder that Pip conceives an almost unconquerable aversion to this man, when even Herbert, unimplicated in Magwitch's wealth (as he fondly believes), shrinks away. Pip's subsequent willingness to detect and honour the goodness in Magwitch's conduct is not a simple recovery from snobbery, but courage of a rare and fine kind. But Pip is dazed by his own misfortunes during this period and enveloped in a nightmare; and when all is finished, he sinks into a fever and almost dies.

—A. E. Dyson, *The Inimitable Dickens: A Study of the Novels* (London: Macmillan, 1970): pp. 238–240.

Q. D. Leavis on Guilt and Class in *Great Expectations*

[Q. D. Leavis (1906–1981) was an important British literary critic. With her husband, F. R. Leavis, she founded the journal *Scrutiny,* and she also wrote the study *Fiction and the Reading Public* (1932). Her *Collected Essays* began publication in 1983. In this extract, Leavis believes the core of *Great Expectations* to lie in its examination of guilt and class-consciousness.]

Dickens's preoccupations in *Great Expectations* are with the fundamental realities of his society and focus on two questions: how was it that a sense of *guilt* was implanted in every child, and with what consequences? And what part does *Class* play in the development of such a member of that society? The novelist is concerned with the effects of these two sanctions, guilt and shame, and it is an inseparable feature of this concern that he constantly insinuates the question: what is 'real' in such a context? for Pip is continually in doubt and perplexity as to whether the real life is that social one with its rules of right and wrong, into which he was born, or the life of the imagination that grows out of natural feeling, into which he was inducted from the opening chapter, his first distinct memory. Of course it is in the working out and presentation of these inquiries that the value of the novel lies, in the minute particularities of the individual life which are yet so skilfully invented as to carry overtones of allegory and to be exemplary. The pertinacity and concentration of Dickens's mind on his theme has made the two questions, in which the third is implied, so interwoven as to be inseparable eventually, and his Shakespearean genius as a creator has produced the wonderful plot which is not only exciting to read and faultless in execution but strikingly classical in its peripeteia. Every detail of the plot, moreover, expresses some aspect, some further aspect, of the theme, and one that is necessary for its full apprehension by the reader. A remarkable feature of the novel is the complexity of the irony which informs the plot from beginning to end (the rewritten end which is demonstrably superior to the one first intended and which perfectly completes the intention and meaning of the novel)—an irony which inheres in the title; yet the novel is affirmative and constructive, not, like other novels shot through with irony (e.g. *Huckleberry Finn, The Confidence Man, Le Rouge et le Noir*), pessimistic or nihilistic.

And whereas Dickens's difficulties, ever since they first appeared in *Oliver Twist*, in reconciling the reader's demands for realism with his own need, for his creative intentions, of a non-rational symbolism of situation and action, a freer form of dealing with experience than his inheritance from the eighteenth-century novelists provided, he has at last, in *Great Expectations,* managed to reconcile realism and symbolism so that in this novel we move without protest, or uneasiness even, from the 'real' world of everyday experience into the non-rational life of the guilty conscience or spiritual experience, outside time and place and with its own logic: somehow we are inhibited from applying the rules of common sense to it even where we hardly recognize that it is symbolic action and can not possibly be plausible real life. The novel is also remarkable for having no wide divergences of prose style either, as even *Bleak House* has; almost the only rhetoric is the passage where Pip tries to explain to Estella his feelings for her, where the effect of weak egotism is required and deliberately obtained through rhetorical language. There is a consistent sobriety of language without losing idiomatic identity for the characters, who range widely nevertheless, as from Jaggers to Joe, from Wemmick to Herbert, from Miss Havisham to Mrs. Joe, and this personal idiom is even what distinguishes Magwitch from Orlick. While Dickens works here, as in *George Silverman's Explanation*, with the minimum in word, setting and characterization, he does not sacrifice in *Great Expectations* scope, range, richness or imaginative complexity. This is the Dickens novel the mature and exigent are now likely to re-read most often and to find more and more in each time, perhaps because it seems to have more relevance outside its own age than any other of Dickens's creative work.

—Q. D. Leavis, "How We Must Read *Great Expectations,*" *Dickens the Novelist* by F. R. Leavis and Q. D. Leavis (London: Chatto & Windus, 1970): pp. 288–289.

JOHN LUCAS ON PIP AS CHARACTER AND PIP AS NARRATOR

[John Lucas is a professor of English and drama at the University of Loughborough in Leicestershire, England. He has written *The Literature of Change* (1977), *England and Englishness* (1990), and other works. In this extract, Lucas points out that Pip as narrator has a different point of view than Pip as a character, and that Pip's own judgment of himself may perhaps be unduly harsh.]

There are essentially two points of view in *Great Expectations*. One is that of the Pip who lives through the novel, the other belongs to the Pip who narrates it. And the second point of view is the authoritative one, commenting on, correcting, judging the earlier self (or selves). To take just one example. When Joe accompanies Pip to Miss Havisham's to speak about the boy's being apprenticed, we are told that he will not talk to Miss Havisham but addresses all his remarks to Pip:

> It was quite in vain for me to endeavour to make him sensible that he ought to speak to Miss Havisham. The more I made faces and gestures to him to do it, the more confidential, argumentative, and polite, he persisted in being to Me.
>
> 'Have you brought his indentures with you?' asked Miss Havisham.
>
> 'Well, Pip, you know,' replied Joe, as if that were a little unreasonable, 'you see me put 'em in my 'at, and therefore you know as they are here.' With which he took them out, and gave them, not to Miss Havisham, but to me. I am afraid I was ashamed of the dear good fellow—I *know* I was ashamed of him—when I saw that Estella stood at the back of Miss Havisham's chair, and that her eyes laughed mischievously. I took the indentures out of his hand and gave them to Miss Havisham.

It is a beautifully caught moment. On the one hand there is the boy's genuine and even perhaps excusable embarrassment. On the other, there is the narrator's self-accusation. And the fineness of the scene—its truth—depends on the way that the acknowledgement of shame is handled. 'I am afraid I was ashamed of the dear good fellow.' That is not shame. It has about it the clear hint of condescension which appeals to the reader to understand that there was every reason for shame. And of course Pip, the man who is launched into society, *does* feel superior to his country relatives, there is no helping it. But there is every helping the self-knowledge that can pass into self-congratulation. Hence the stern—'I *know* I was ashamed of him.' The qualification acts as a rebuke to the previous lightly accepted culpability. It shows that the narrator is determined to get at the real truth.

I have made heavy weather of what is a fairly simple matter. Yet it is worth emphasizing how sternly Pip wishes to judge himself and his life. All signs of self-pity and complacency are rooted out as they become identified.

But this brings us to an interesting point. The severity of Pip's self-judgement may eventually prove to be in excess of what he has to show us of his life. In other words, there is a third point of view that *Great Expectations* allows for—ours. Almost the best thing about the novel is that because of the self-excoriating quality with which Pip is determined to tell the truth about himself, we understand that his desire to atone for past errors leads him to identify error where none exists. There must be no hint of a desire for martyrdom about this, or the novel will be ruined. Dickens's success depends on his making Pip's desire for atonement plausible and honourable, not priggish or coy. And by and large the success is guaranteed because in spite of Pip's faults we are persuaded of his honesty, candour and essential likeability. Because, although it is proper that he should regard the course of his life as dictated by faults, it is also proper that we should see the matter otherwise. In particular, the novel makes us understand that great expectations are highly problematic. Can one even be guilty of entertaining them, or are they inevitably fed into people's lives?

—John Lucas, *The Melancholy Man: A Study of Dickens's Novels* (London: Methuen, 1970): pp. 290–292.

[Pearl Chesler Solomon is a professor of teacher education at St. Thomas Aquinas College in Sparkill, New York,
and author of *Dickens and Melville in Their Time* (1975),
from which the following extract is taken. Here, Solomon
examines the shift of focus in Dickens's work from *David
Copperfield* to *Great Expectations*, noting that in the
interval Dickens has come to terms with his feelings for
his own father.]

Sometime after his father's death, Dickens said of him, "The longer I
live, the better man I think him." In the fragment of autobiography
written long before John Dickens's death, Dickens blamed his
father's neglect of himself on two faults, ease of temper and straitness of means, and as long as his father lived, Dickens continued to
be annoyed by the consequences of these traits. But in *Great Expectations* ease of temper and straitness of means are not incompatible
with great virtue. They are, in fact, attributes of the saintly man who
was Pip's first father, Joe Gargery. Joe's passivity and poverty in no
way harm the child, while his love and protection save him. Dickens
seems to be saying now that the blacking warehouse was not the central crisis of his childhood as the blacksmith's forge was not the central crisis of Pip's. The crisis of Pip's childhood has nothing to do
with money or class, but with love. Pip's hell is the absence of love,
and it is the sister who takes the place of his mother, and who bears
his mother's name, who makes that hell. In some such way as this,
Dickens reassessed the events of his own past to make the father his
deliverer, his mother his would-be destroyer. The central issue in this
reconsideration of his past is, again, the source of love. It was love
that saved Pip from Magwitch's fate: his father's love, Joe Gargery's.

So bent is Dickens upon making the principal source of Pip's guilt
his criminal ingratitude toward Joe that he entirely removes David's
reason for feeling guilty toward his father—the desire he felt for possession of his mother. Pip cannot feel desire for Mrs. Joe, whose
embattled bosom, stuck full of pins, repels the advance of all living
creatures. It is Joe's second wife who is like Clara Copperfield; who is
young and gentle and loving; and who is the object of Orlick's (and
therefore of Pip's) lust. But Pip represses his lust for Biddy—is not

guilty of even fantasy incest with the woman who will become Joe's wife. And toward the child of Biddy and Joe, the child who is also named Pip, the older Pip will see Joe free to become a better father—the father Mrs. Joe prevented Joe from being to him.

Pip's redemption begins when he realizes that he must renounce Magwitch's money partly because it now seems to him criminal to live on unearned money, partly because, in some narrowly moralistic way, Pip doesn't deserve it. But there is a sense in which Pip doesn't get Magwitch's money because he deserves something better than a criminal's patrimony. By means of Pip's association with Magwitch, Dickens is reassessing once more the blacking warehouse experience. It is through Magwitch and Magwitch's money that Pip is dragged to the borderline of the criminal underworld, and Pip must reject both the man and his money in order to remain a "gentleman." What Pip has *earned* from Magwitch, Dickens seems to feel, is the right to respectable employment. What he has been given unearned, again, is an education. And it is this education which was Magwitch's gift to him, along with the unearned love which was Joe's gift, which together "fathered" Pip, and which made of him a true gentleman.

—Pearl Chesler Solomon, *Dickens and Melville in Their Time* (New York: Columbia University Press, 1975): pp. 168–171.

⊛

MURRAY BAUMGARTEN ON WRITING AND SPEECH IN *GREAT EXPECTATIONS*

[Murray Baumgarten is a professor of general literature at the University of California at Santa Cruz. He has written *City Scriptures: Modern Jewish Writing* (1982) and *Understanding Philip Roth* (1990). In this extract, Baumgarten studies *Great Expectations* in the context of Dickens's stenographic activities as a reporter, showing that these activities helped to break down the distinction between writing and speech in Dickens's mind and in the minds of his readers.]

By the time he published *Great Expectations* in serial form in 1860–1861, Dickens had already written twelve novels, edited four magazines for which he had written at least a million words, and published two books of travel and social observation. He was forty-nine years old.

He began his career as a court reporter and transcriber of Parliamentary debates, which he reproduced for newspaper publication with phenomenal speed and accuracy. Like Pip, Dickens had taught himself to read and write; like David Copperfield he had taught himself to take shorthand before he was sixteen, very quickly becoming the best stenographer of his time. As Steven Marcus points out in a classic article, this talent of Dickens' helped make it possible for him to recast the conventional relation between speech and writing.

Once he had mastered the stenographic characters in a process that receives brilliant description in Chapter 38 of *David Copperfield,* they were no longer the constituents of an imprisoning code, Marcus points out, but the playful doodles of speech. The stenographic "characters, as he describes them in recollection, were themselves doodles—apparently random plays of the pen, out of which figures or partial figures would emerge and to which meaning could be ascribed." As a result, speech could "now be rendered not only in the abstract forms of cursive or printed letters and units; it could be represented *graphically* as well." Marcus emphasizes that this "experience of an alternative, quasi-graphic way of representing speech had among other things the effect upon Dickens of loosening up the rigid relations between speech and writing that prevail in our linguistic and cultural system." These flourishes of the pen, these squiggles and doodles, provided Dickens "with an experience of something that closely resembled a hieroglyphic means of preserving speech," making it possible for "the spoken language to enter into his writing with a parity it had never enjoyed before in English fictional prose. Speech here was not the traditional subordinate of its written representation; it could appear now in writing with a freedom and spontaneity that made it virtually, if momentarily, writing's equal." Dramatizing the acquisition of literacy in *Great Expectations,* and revealing the gulf between oral and written culture, Dickens occupies a particularly heady moment in western cultural history. He can look both ways, and bring into the future alphabetic code of the west the childhood experience of calligraphy, when the alphabetic character is both phoneme and picture.

In this novel as was the case throughout the nineteenth century, most reading was reading aloud; then writing must be the (sometimes) private act of making the characters that provide a public voice. Perhaps the act of decoding in which we are engaged parallel to that of the characters of *Great Expectations* will lead us as well to the greater magic of encoding—so that we like them may inscribe our selves in the world in which they too are circumscribed. Then our story would become more than a private possession, and be changed into public meaning. Like money that Wemmick refers to as portable property, our story would have added to the store of language and become something from which, like capital, we could all benefit.

Reading *Great Expectations* aloud, we become one of its community of readers. We are the witnesses to its experience. As Pip speaks to us we are not imprisoned in the code of reading, but rather liberated by calligraphic impulses; the characters of the novel, both alphabetic and fictive, are writ large as our meaning. We envision the scene, encounter the portrayed situation, and believe in this rendered world, for it is a true story. In referring to Marcus, I do not mean to make *Great Expectations* into an avatar of *Pickwick Papers*. Rather, it is to emphasize that our experience in reading this novel is not just Pip's deciphering of a code—not mere transcription—but the rhythm of participating in its production. Thereby, we share in a particular version of calligraphic experience. *Great Expectations* gives writing the qualities of speech, the flow of language unceasing and unending. We are sorry when it stops.

—Murray Baumgarten, "Calligraphy and Code: Writing in *Great Expectations*," *Dickens Studies Annual* 11 (1983): pp. 69–70.

THOMAS LOE ON THE GOTHIC ELEMENTS IN *GREAT EXPECTATIONS*

[Thomas Loe is a professor of English at the State University of New York College at Oswego. In this extract, Loe believes that *Great Expectations* is an amalgam of three types of novel: the *Bildungsroman*, or the novel of development from childhood to adulthood; the novel of manners; and the Gothic novel of terror and the supernatural. Loe focuses on this third type, drawing parallels between Dickens's work and Ann Radcliffe's *The Italian* (1797).]

The Gothic novel plot of *The Italian* fits the literal circumstances of the action of *Great Expectations* very closely, and, even though subdued by the *Bildungsroman* and novel of manners plots that dominate the first two stages of Pip's story, this plot initiates the action of the novel and emerges in the final stage to unify and conclude the novel. Some specific parallels could even be argued to exist between the two novels if not pressed too far: Pip resembles both the persecuted Ellena and Vivaldi in his passivity and innocence; Miss Havisham, in her dedication to revenge, resembles the plotting Marchesa; Magwitch and Schedoni have similar roles as accomplices to Compeyson and Nicola, and their ultimate exposures of one another and their deaths are also similar; both books have henchmen like Orlick and Spalatro, who figure in the final explanations about the suspicions of persecution that permeate the novels; and Estella's relationship as daughter to Magwitch is very much like the father-daughter relationship thought to exist between Ellena and Schedoni. The most important structural similarity, though, is the way crime and two shadowy criminals, Nicola and Compeyson, lurk in the backgrounds of the plots in both novels. In *Great Expectations* these archvillains function as they do for the Gothic novel in general: they provide memorable, smoothly coherent actions by allowing the malignant effect of an original evil to be traced through cliff-hanging interruptions. Crime, the manifestation of this evil, is the major metaphor of this plot for all Gothic novels. "That evil genius" Compeyson, despite his only occasional, furtive presence, is the emblematic character for crime and the prime mover of the Gothic plot which eventually ties together all the major lines of action in *Great Expectations*.

So, although Compeyson and his crimes have been taken to task by critics because they are obscure in the first two thirds of the novel and then blatant and melodramatic, it is from their very obscurity that they derive their forcefulness and eventual dominance in the structure of the novel. Dickens begins the action with the intrusion of Magwitch and Compeyson into the formative starting point of Pip's life, his "first most vivid and broad impression of the identity of things," which becomes interwoven with the images of crime, convicts, guilt, and terror which characterize his narrative. Magwitch and Miss Havisham, as well as Estella, Pip, and Jaggers, are important participants in this hidden Gothic plot, and even Orlick's mysterious behind-the-scenes actions are enveloped in his associations of Compeyson. The effect of Pip's imagination working on the associations he has with Orlick, for example, heighten his reaction to the glimpses and reports of a "lurker" he gets prowling around his lodgings. This response parallels and presages the more awful "terror" generated later by the presence of Compeyson, who is revealed by Mr. Wopsle to have sat behind Pip in the theater: "I cannot exaggerate the enhanced disquiet into which this conversation threw me, or the special and peculiar terror I felt as Compeyson's having been behind me 'like a ghost.'" The "special and peculiar" effect is created largely because it is a secret and internalized one. It is an interior effect, a psychological one, created by an imaginative reaction to events, rather than the actual events themselves. Robert Heilman has shown how the similar Gothic accoutrements of *Jane Eyre* create an internalized heightened response in that novel. This same principle of obscurity, so skillfully utilized by Ann Radcliffe, employs Pip's internalized fears to create links between the various plots in *Great Expectations*. Compeyson's crimes against Miss Havisham and Magwitch are created before the time that the novel opens, and the consequences that are visited upon Pip and Estella by their distorted donors are greatly removed from the times and scenes of the crime itself. It is these removed actions that have to be sorted out retrospectively, making the gothic plot resemble a detective plot.

From a retrospective perspective the Gothic plot appears straightforward, like the evil behind it. It consists of Pip's initial help to Magwitch and Magwitch's subsequent attempt to play patron to Pip. Magwitch tries to revenge himself against the society he feels is responsible for his criminal fall and subsequent prosecution, linked in his mind with Compeyson. The parallel plot of Estella is created by Miss Havisham in revenge against men for being deserted by Compeyson. Both plot motivations are bound tightly with Compeyson's evil. Although overlaid in the first two thirds of the novel by the *Bildungsroman* plot and the novel of manners plot, the Gothic plot is kept active by interspersed, brief, but important, reminders of its presence, such as the man stirring his rum-and-water with a file or the later indirect encounter with this same emissary on a stage coach. Fear-inspiring Gothic imagery connected with death, decay, violence, and mental distortions support such actions, and foreshadow the eruption of the Gothic plot with Magwitch's appearance in Chapter Thirty-nine, in what Pip calls "the turning point of my life." Locating the stories and motivations and sorting out the connections between Compeyson, Magwitch, Miss Havisham, Arthur Havisham, and Jaggers make up the rest of the Gothic plot. These correspond generally with the separate plot lines that are played off against one another by creating expectations for the reader, and then interrupted with another story. Even though the plotting and actions leading up to the final river flight and its aftermath are often regarded as "one of the highest achievements of the sensation novel" (Lionel Stevenson), they are integrally bound with the deliberate obscurity of the main Gothic plot that flows, subdued or dominant, throughout the novel. What has been deliberately concealed is finally revealed for maximum effect. This third type of plot is also bound closely with the change of heart that Pip has towards Magwitch, the last important development of his *Bildungsroman* plot, and with the concurrent collapse of his social aspirations inspired by his idealization of Estella, the motivation behind the novel of manners plot.

—Thomas Loe, "Gothic Plot in *Great Expectations*," *Dickens Quarterly* 6, no. 3 (September 1989): pp. 107–109.

Plot Summary of
Bleak House

In the **first chapter** of *Bleak House* Dickens sets forth his social criticism and one of the book's main themes: the Chancery Court, with its costs and lawyer's fees, ruins people's lives. The court is in session and preparing to hear some part of the case of Jarndyce and Jarndyce. The Lord High Chancellor will consider making "two young people" (Ada Clare and Richard Carstone) wards of their cousin (John Jarndyce). The case is an old one and "has become so complicated that no man alive knows what it means."

Lady Dedlock, in London before leaving for Paris, consults her lawyer, Mr. Tulkinghorn, who represents her interests in the Jarndyce and Jarndyce matter (**chapter two**). She becomes curious about the handwriting on some papers Tulkinhorn has brought along. A few moments later, she nearly faints.

At the Chancery Court (**chapter three**) Esther Summerson meets Ada Clare and Richard Carstone. The three, all now wards of Mr. Jarndyce, become friends. As they leave the court, they encounter an old woman who seems to have been driven mad by the never-ending tangle of the Jarndyce and Jarndyce suit. Continuing on their journey to Bleak House, the three friends wonder what sort of man Mr. Jarndyce might be (**chapter four**). Esther, Ada, and Richard arrive at Bleak House and meet the benevolent Mr. Jarndyce, at last. Esther is eager to begin her duties as housekeeper (**chapter six**).

Chapter seven describes gloomy and mysterious circumstances that seem to foreshadow the misfortune the Dedlocks will endure. At Chesney Wold, the Dedlock country estate, a visitor tells the story of the Ghost's Walk: In Oliver Cromwell's time, Sir Morbury Dedlock's wife had deliberately lamed some horses intended for the Cavaliers fighting against Cromwell. Mowbry caught her as she was about to lame another horse. They fought, and she herself was painfully lamed in the struggle. Later, she died, vowing to haunt the estate until "the pride of [Chesney Wold] is humbled."

In **chapter eight** Esther learns that the lawsuit in which she is involved centers around a will that had promised a considerable fortune. Now, however, there is nothing left of the money; Chancery court costs have consumed everything. Tom Jarndyce, the former owner of Bleak House, after trying for many years to settle the suit, had shot himself.

Esther and Ada accompany a charity worker, Mrs. Pardiggle, to the home of an impoverished bricklayer. A boy dies while they are there. They are as shocked by Mrs. Pardiggle's aggressive attitude toward the family as they are by the squalor of the home. Here, as he does throughout the novel, Dickens satirizes the professional social activist. Mrs. Pardiggle's self-absorbed shallowness contrasts the genuine concern of Esther and Ada toward the family.

Mr. Jarndyce tries to secure a job for Richard Carstone, but the young man's restlessness and indecisiveness has left him unprepared for any position. Meanwhile, Esther becomes convinced that Richard and Ada are in love (**chapter nine**).

In **chapters ten** and **eleven** Mr. Tulkinghorn seeks to identify the handwriting on several Jarndyce and Jarndyce documents. The handwriting belongs to Mr. Nemo (Latin for "no one"), a pauper who has just died of opium poisoning. After an inquest, at which Jo, a street sweeper, asserts that Nemo had been kind to him, Nemo's death is ruled an accident. After a ridiculous inquest into the circumstances of his death, by which Dickens satirizes legal procedures, Nemo is buried as a pauper in a dreary churchyard. Tulkinghorn realizes that Lady Dedlock is more than "casually" interested when he tells her about the handwriting that had interested her (**chapter twelve**). She insists on hearing the entire story of Nemo's death.

In **chapter thirteen** Mr. Jarndyce finds Richard Carstone a position as a surgeon's apprentice. Richard and Ada realize that they are in love, and Esther finds herself attracted to Allan Woodcourt, a young surgeon. Richard pursues his career, but believes that the Chancery suit will yet make him rich (**chapter fourteen**).

Lady Dedlock, disguised as a maid, seeks out Jo in London (**chapter sixteen**). The street sweeper shows her where Nemo died. At Chesney Wold there is talk that the "step on the Ghost's Walk" has never been "more distinct than it is tonight." The reader wonders why Lady Dedlock is interested in the dead pauper. In **chapter seventeen**, Esther's increasing curiosity about her own past parallels Lady Dedlock's interest in Nemo.

By **chapter eighteen**, Richard has abandoned medical apprenticeship for a career in law. In church, Esther is astonished at the resemblance between Lady Dedlock and Miss Barbary. Later, as Lady Dedlock speaks, Esther feels a surprising connection: ". . . there arose before my mind innumerable pictures of myself." Lady Dedlock offends her French maid, Mlle. Hortense, a violent woman who will later extract her revenge.

Mr. Tulkinghorn finds out that Lady Dedlock had made inquiries about Nemo. He hires a detective to find Jo, who confirms the report (**chapter twenty-two**). In comparison to the revolting character of the lawyer, Tulkinghorn, Lady Dedlock is a person of high character.

In **chapter twenty-four** Richard has abandoned both his apprenticeship and his engagement to Ada for an officer's commission in the army. His leaving Ada foreshadows his early death.

As cold weather approaches, the Dedlocks leave Chesney Wold for their home in London (**chapter twenty-nine**). Tulkinghorn is a frequent visitor, much to Lady Dedlock's discomfort. A law clerk comes to tell her that she may be interested in knowing that Esther Summerson's father was Captain Hawdon (Nemo). Lady Dedlock realizes that her daughter is alive; that her sister, Miss Barbary, had lied about the child's death.

Esther finds a place for Jo, who is ill, apparently with smallpox (**chapter thirty-one**). Esther contracts the disease and is temporarily blinded. She recovers after several weeks, but her face is left scarred (**chapter thirty-five**). Richard, ever self-destructive, has convinced himself that Mr. Jarndyce is his rival in the Jarndyce and Jarndyce suit. Esther learns that Allan Woodcourt has saved many lives in a shipwreck.

Lady Dedlock reveals to Esther that she is her mother (**chapter thirty-six**). She asks her to forgive her and to keep this knowledge a secret. She gives Esther a letter, telling her to destroy it after she has read it. She advises Esther to beware of the suspicious Tulkinghorn. Esther reads, then burns, the letter. Later, on the Ghost's Walk, Esther feels that she has brought "calamity on the stately house" of Dedlock. The next afternoon, Ada arrives and they are happily reunited.

In the midst of a chapter satirizing British party politics (**chapter forty**), Tulkinghorn tells Sir Leicester the story, without using any names, of Esther, Lady Dedlock, and Captain Hawdon. Lady Dedlock betrays no more that a casual interest, and her self-control and dignity is in sharp contrast to the lawyer's viciousness.

In **chapter forty-one** Lady Dedlock confronts Tulkinghorn, demanding to know why he has told so many people her story. The lawyer tells her that he wanted her to know that he knew her secret. She suggests that she will leave Chesney Wold but she does not want to bring pain to Sir Leicester. Since he doesn't quite know what to do with his knowledge of Lady Dedlock's secret, Tulkinghorn tells her that he will tell no one the truth. The next morning Tulkinghorn seems "at his oldest . . . as if the digger and the spade were both commissioned, and would soon be digging." In **chapter forty-eight** he is found dead, "shot through the heart." Detective Bucket arrests George Rouncewell, the son of the Dedlock's housekeeper at Chesney Wold, for Tulkinghorn's murder (**chapter forty-nine**).

In **chapter fifty** Allan Woodcourt and Esther meet frequently and their relationship becomes closer. She tells Ada that Mr. Jarndyce has proposed marriage, and is puzzled by "a quiet sorrow" she notices in her friend. Allan, meanwhile, has visited Richard and found him dejected, having made no progress with the Chancery suit—and no progress toward his fortune (**chapter fifty-one**). Ada, with "tears in her eyes and love in her face," confesses to Esther that she and Richard have been married two months and that she will not be returning to Bleak House. Esther tells Mr. Jarndyce who remarks that "Bleak House is thinning fast." Ada's future is now inevitably intertwined with Richard's.

Dickens returns to the detective story in **chapter fifty-two**. Esther, Allan, and Mr. Jarndyce visit George in prison. He tells Mr. Jarndyce that on the night of the murder, he saw a figure pass him on the dark stairs.

Detective Bucket tells an astonished Sir Leicester that his wife is a suspect in the murder. He learns of his wife's relationship with Captain Hawdon, of her visit to his grave, and of the "bad blood" between her and Tulkinghorn (**chapters fifty-three** and **fifty-four**). Bucket arrests Mlle. Hortense for murder after he deduces her relationship with Tulkinghorn and her appearance in Lady Dedlock's clothes. Bucket has recovered the gun Hortense had thrown into the lake. The shock of all this causes Sir Leicester to suffer a stroke.

Lacking vital information—that her husband has forgiven her; that Hortense has been arrested—Lady Dedlock writes a letter to Sir Leicester in which she states that, while she did not kill Tulkinghorn, she is probably guilty of everything else he "[has] heard, or will hear." She leaves all money and jewels behind as she leaves the house (**chapter fifty-five**). Sir Leicester sends Detective Bucket to find her. Mr. Jarndyce allows Esther to accompany Bucket in his search for her mother (**chapter fifty-six**). They find Lady Dedlock, "cold and dead," at the gate of the paupers' cemetery where Captain Hawdon is buried.

In **chapter sixty** Esther falls ill and is attended by Allan. Ada, now pregnant, lives in poverty with Richard who has lost all ambition and hope for the future. Ada fears that Richard will not live long enough to see the child. We are here prepared for imminent death of Richard and for the engagement of Esther and Allan.

By **chapter sixty-four** Mr. Jarndyce realizes that his engagement to Esther must give way to the love that has grown between Esther and Allan. He releases her from her promise to marry him and settles Allan in "a new Bleak House." Esther is astonished to realize that she will still become "the mistress of Bleak House" not as Mr. Jarndyce's wife, but as Allan's.

Chapters sixty-five and **sixty-six** bring the lawsuit and its effects on those involved to a close. Court costs are revealed to have taken the entire estate. Richard, already ill, dies the same day.

Seven years later (**chapter sixty-seven**) Esther and Allan are happy at Bleak House with two daughters; Ada, with her son born shortly after Richard's death, lives at the "older" Bleak House with Mr. Jarndyce. According to Allan, Esther is prettier than ever. Goodness triumphs. ❀

List of Characters in
Bleak House

Lady Honoria Dedlock is the charming, beautiful, and very vain wife of Sir Leicester and mother of Esther Summerson, the protagonist of the novel. Although she initiates or is otherwise involved in most of the action of the novel, she is a comparatively undeveloped character about whose inner life we learn very little. She has a secret unknown even to her husband: When young, she had born an illegitimate daughter to her lover, Captain Hawdon.

Esther Summerson is a ward of Mr. Jarndyce and the illegitimate daughter of Lady Dedlock and Captain Hawdon. She is both narrator and protagonist of most of the story. Raised from birth by her "godmother," who is actually her aunt (Miss Barbary), then John Jarndyce, after her aunt's death, Esther is now twenty years old. She is a virtuous, virginal young woman, educated at a boarding school, returned to Bleak House to serve in Mr. Jarndyce's household.

John Jarndyce is the kindly owner of Bleak House—which is not bleak at all—and the legal guardian of Esther Summerson, Richard Carstone, and Ada Clare. He is a "stock" character whose function in the novel is to act as protector and benefactor to those less fortunate than himself. Like Lady Dedlock, he seems to have no interior life.

Mr. Tulkinghorn is Sir Leicester Dedlock's chief legal counsel; solicitor of the Chancery Court. He is arrogant, cunning, vengeful, and determined to discover Lady Dedlock's secret. As Esther is the protagonist, he is the antagonist of the novel. His ruthless pursuit of Lady Dedlock's secret gives the impression that, more than the protection of his client's, Sir Leicester's interests, he enjoys wielding a sadistic power over her.

Richard Carstone is cousin to Ada Clare and a ward of Mr. Jarndyce. With Ada Clare and Mr. Jarndyce, he is involved in a convoluted lawsuit ("Jarndyce and Jarndyce") that has consumed nearly all of an inheritance. He is youthfully optimistic and enthusiastic, but also impractical and utterly irresponsible.

Ada Clare is a close friend of Esther Summerson. Both are beautiful and virtuous young woman; Esther, too, is a ward of Mr. Jarndyce, orphaned and serving in the household. Through the confidences she and Esther share we learn at least a little about their characters. Unlike Richard, she is prudent and practical.

Sir Leicester Dedlock is an aristocrat and owner of Chesney Wold, his ancestral estate in Lincolnshire. He becomes, in many ways, the most interesting character in the novel. He changes over the course of the story, actively engaging himself in his sorrows, friendships, and in his bereavement after the death of his wife. ❀

Critical Views on
Bleak House

J. HILLIS MILLER ON THE THEME OF INTERPRETATION
IN THE NOVEL

[J. Hillis Miller is Professor of Victorian Literature at the
University of California, Irvine. He is a noted literary critic;
author of *Charles Dickens: The World of His Novels, Theory
Now and Then*, and *Ariadne's Thread: Story Lines, and
Topographies*. In this extract, Miller discusses interpretations
that the novel's characters make about one another, and
shows how they are often false.]

Some of the most dreamlike and grotesque episodes in the novel
involve documents, for example, the chapter in which Grandfather
Smallweed, after Krook's death, rummages among the possessions
of the deceased, surrounded, in his chair, with great piles of paper,
or the chilling scene of the end of Jarndyce and Jarndyce. The latter
moves beyond 'realism' in the usual sense toward what Baudelaire
in 'The Essence of Laughter' calls the 'dizzy hyperbole' of the
'absolute comic':

> It appeared to be something that made the professional
> gentlemen very merry, for there were several young coun-
> sellors in wigs and whiskers on the outside of the crowd,
> and when one of them told the others about it, they put
> their hands in their pockets, and quite doubled them-
> selves up with laughter, and went stamping about the
> pavement of the Hall . . . [P]resently great bundles of
> papers began to be carried out—bundles in bags, bundles
> too large to be got into any bags, immense masses of
> papers of all shapes and no shapes, which the bearers
> staggered under, and threw down for the time being,
> anyhow, on the Hall pavement, while they went back to
> bring out more. Even these clerks were laughing.

Not to put too fine a point upon it, as Mr Snagsby would say, what
is the meaning of all this hermeneutical and archival activity? The
reader of the novel must go beyond surface appearances to the
deeper coherences of which these surfaces are the dispersed signs. In

the same way, many of the characters are cryptographers. They attempt to fit details together to make a pattern revealing some hidden secret. Like Krook they must put 'J' and 'a' and so on together to spell 'Jarndyce'. They want to identify the buried truth which is the substance behind all the shadowy signs which they are surrounded, as Richard Carstone believes that there 'is—is—must be somewhere' 'truth and justice' in the case of Jarndyce and Jarndyce. Two motives impel these readers of signs. Like Richard, Gridley or even, in spite of herself, Esther, they may want to find out secrets about themselves. Each seeks his unrevealed place in the system of which he is a part. To find out how I am related to others will be to find out who I am, for I am defined by my connections, familial or legal. Esther *is* the illegitimate daughter of Lady Dedlock and Captain Hawdon. Richard *is,* or perhaps is not, a rightful heir to the Jarndyce fortune. Other characters—Mr Tulkinghorn, Guppy, Grandfather Smallweed, Hortense, Mrs Snagsby or Inspector Bucket —want to find out secrets about others. Their motive is the search for power. To find out the hidden place of another in the system is to be able to manipulate him, to dominate him, of course to make money out of him.

These two versions of the theme of interpretation echo through the novel in melodramatic and parodic forms. Many characters find themselves surrounded by mysterious indications, sinister, threatening or soliciting. Poor Mr Snagsby says, 'I find myself wrapped round with secrecy and mystery, till my life is a burden to me'. He is 'a party to some dangerous secret, without knowing what it is. And it is the fearful peculiarity of this condition that, at any hour of his daily life, . . . the secret may take air and fire, explode, and blow up'. Most of the characters are more aggressive than Mr Snagsby in their relation to secrets. Mr Tulkinghorn's 'calling is the acquisition of secrets, and the holding possession of such power as they give him, with no sharer or opponent in it'. Guppy slowly puts together the evidence of Lady Dedlock's guilt and Esther's parentage. 'It's going on,' he says of his 'case,' 'and I shall gather it up closer and closer as it goes on'. In the same way, Hortense, Lady Dedlock's maid, is 'maliciously watchful . . . of everyone and everything', and the 'one occupation' of Mrs Snagsby's jealous life 'has been . . . to follow Mr Snagsby to and fro, and up and down, and to piece suspicious circumstances together'. She has, says Mr Bucket, 'done a deal more harm in bringing odds and ends together than if she had meant it'.

Just as Gridley, Richard and Miss Flute are obsessed with the documents in their 'cases', so the Smallweeds carry on Krook's search for valuable papers after his death, 'rummaging and searching, digging, delving, and diving among the treasures of the late lamented'. Tom Jarndyce, the original owner of Bleak House, who finally blew out his brains in despair, lived there, 'shut up: day and night poring over the wicked heaps of papers in the suit, and hoping against hope to disentangle it from its mystification and bring it to a close'. Even Sir Leicester, when he hears the story of a noble lady unfaithful to her husband, 'arranges a sequence of events on a plan of his own', and Esther, though she makes no detective effort to uncover the facts about her birth, nevertheless finds Lady Dedlock's face, 'in a confused way, like a broken glass to me, in which I saw scraps of old remembrances'. She is, in spite of herself, led to put these broken pieces together to mirror the truth about herself, just as, in relation to another secret, she says, 'I observed it in many slight particulars, which were nothing in themselves, and only became something when they were pieced together'.

The remarkable fact is that these interpreters for the most part are failures. Sometimes their interpretations are false, fictional patterns thrown over the surface of things like a mirage without relation to any deeper truth. Sometimes authentic secrets are discovered but are found out too late or in the wrong way to be of any use to their discoverers. *Bleak House* is full of unsuccessful detectives. The 'plan of his own' which Sir Leicester constructs does not save him from the revelation which will shatter his proud complacency. Mrs Snagsby is ludicrously mistaken in her idea that her husband has been unfaithful and is the father of Jo. Krook dies before he finds anything of value in his papers, and even Grandfather Smallweed makes little out of his discovery. Guppy finds out Lady Dedlock's secret, but it does not win him Esther's hand. Gridley dies without resolving his suit. The case of Jarndyce and Jarndyce is used up in costs before the revelation of the newly discovered will which might have brought it to a close. Even Tulkinghorn and Bucket, the two most clairvoyant and persistent detectives in the novel, are failures. Tulkinghorn is murdered just before he is going to make use of the secret he has discovered about Lady Dedlock. Bucket, in spite of the fact that 'the velocity and certainty of [his] interpretation . . . is little short of miraculous', does not save Lady Dedlock. The masterly intuition which leads him to see that she has changed clothes with the brickmaker's wife (another lateral displacement) gets Esther to her mother just too late. They find her 'cold and dead' on the steps of Nemo's graveyard. Moreover, the novel is deliberately constructed by Dickens in a way calculated to make the reader a bad detective. Carefully placed cues are designed to lead the reader to believe that either George Rouncewell or Lady Dedlock has murdered Tulkinghorn. Even now, when Dickens's strewing of false clues may seem amateur in comparison with the sophisticated puzzles in modern mystery stories, some readers, one may imagine, are inveigled into thinking that Lady Dedlock is a murderess.

—J. Hillis Miller, "Dickens's Bleak House." In Charles Dickens, ed. Steven Connor (New York: Longman, 1996): pp. 64–66.

VIRGINIA BLAIN ON ESTHER'S "SEXUAL TAINT"

[Virginia Blain is the author of *Caroline Bowles Southey: The Making of a Woman Writer, A Feminist Companion to Literature in English, Women's Poetry in the Enlightenment: The Making of a Canon,* and *Women's Poetry: Late Romantic to Late Victorian: Gender and Genre, 1830–1900.* In this extract, she discusses sexual repression in Bleak House.]

The sexual taint on Esther (as Dickens shows) is bestowed on her not by her mother's act so much as by the hostility to women endemic in a patriarchal society. It is this taint which sets her invisibly apart from other women and yet at the same time makes her their archetypal representative. This is because she bears within her as a deeply-buried wound the guilt and shame that the position of women in such a society inflicts on all females to some degree. None the less, her 'inheritance of shame' as she aptly terms it can only be expunged at the cost of her joining with the patriarchy, the world of men, of male legality and legitimacy, and to to do this effectively she has to cast off her mother. And this is precisely what she does, in my reading, by joining forces with Mr Bucket in the death-chase of Lady Dedlock. Readers have long felt the power of this climactic chase, while being at the same time rather at a loss to account for its resonance in a novel about Chancery. I want now to offer a reading which suggests that Dickens's unerring dramatic instincts have here a deeper basis than has hitherto been suspected. This part of the novel takes on a wider significance when we realise the importance of the submerged tensions of sexual repression and vengeance which underpin it.

That Tulkinghorn and his avenger Bucket are both agents of a judicial system which has been exposed in the novel as an instrument of vengeance, and are both at the same time so strongly identified with the masculine ethic of the society, makes them fitting accomplices in the purgation of 'illicit' female sexuality through the sacrifice of Lady Dedlock along with her surrogate, Hortense. Taylor Stoehr has argued that the chief weakness of the split point of view in *Bleak House* is that the two themes (Esther's sexual-social dilemma and Richard's vocational one) are never brought into meaningful contact with each other. But in my view the ultimate effect of the split narrative is, on the contrary, finally to enforce a connection, by pressing the analogy between the separate male and female spheres until they achieve climactic union in the expulsion of Lady Dedlock, who is used very precisely, in Girard's terms, as a ritual sacrificial victim or scapegoat for the transferred hostilities within a patriarchal society.

It has often been remarked that it is in the pursuit of Lady Dedlock that the two narratives draw together. Esther in her role as female voice has always been time-bound in her narration; it is the male narrator who can command the 'timeless' present tense. But now for the first time, the two narratives 'coincide in their focusing of time and space at the end of Chapter 56' as Stoehr reminds us. He continues.

> Bucket, who has appeared in Esther's narrative only once, is now taken into her story completely, as he and Esther rush through the countryside in pursuit of Lady Dedlock. This chapter and the next but one, both told from Esther's point of view, bring us to the gates of the burial ground, which also figures in Esther's narrative now for the first time, and Lady Dedlock is thus brought into her daughter's story, and out of the present-tense narrative, for good and all. The whole sequence, in which *single* chapters from the two narratives alternate for the first time in the novel, is constructed as a joining of the points of view *in order to bring Esther and her mother together.*

It is this conclusion that I feel constrained to question, yet it is the conclusion most commonly drawn from this part of the novel. John Lucas spells it out even more clearly in his book on Dickens, *The Melancholy Man* (London, 1970), where he writes:

> Esther's narrative . . . has to do with what seem to be entirely different matters and yet all the while is moving closer to the other narrative, until there is a total fusion of the two in the *girl's reunion with the mother who has denied her.*

What kind of a 'reunion' can Esther possibly have with a dead body? The mother is not only 'cold and dead' when discovered by her daughter, but also in one of those disguises which is perhaps not so much a disguise as a revelation of true identity, the clothes of the more obvious social outcast, that other 'distressed, unsheltered' creature, Jenny, the brickmaker's wife, whom Esther now tellingly 'recognises' as 'the mother of the dead child'. For surely it is the childish Esther herself who has now 'died' to her mother, in order to live again—to live 'legitimately'—as a woman in that very society which has made of her mother a scapegoat to purge its own sins of violence, both sexual and social. Esther, in a sense, has to 'kill' her mother within herself, in order to escape her contagion. The chase by Bucket, with the passive collusion of Esther, ostensibly to 'save' Lady Dedlock, has in fact resulted in her death—since the more relentless their pursuit, the more desperate her flight, and the more inevitable her end. In fulfilling the role of surrogate victim for society's guilty violence, Lady Dedlock beautifully illustrates by her melodramatic death what Gerald observes in his book to be the 'fundamental identity' of 'vengeance, sacrifice and legal punishment'.

As Girard cogently argues, the whole notion of legitimacy has grown up in our society linked with religion as a means of containing violent impulses. Sexuality is 'impure' because it has to do with violence, not the other way about, and Girard notes the possibility of 'some half-suppressed desire in men to place the blame for all forms of violence on women'. Sir Leicester may forgive his wife her sexual transgression (once he is paralysed, and she at the point of death); none the less it is deeply necessary to the mythic shape of the novel that Lady Dedlock suffer and die, cast out from society. Her punishment must exceed her 'crime' for her function as ritual victim, or scapegoat, to be fulfilled. It is only by virtue of the relative innocence of a scapegoat that it can take on the burden of others' guilts. The expulsion of the scapegoat is not only part of a purification ritual, but vital in preventing violence from escalating through reciprocated acts of vengeance.

By the very act of showing Lady Dedlock as a scapegoat figure, Dickens indicates what lay just as deep and hidden in him as any horror of female power or female sexuality: a knowledge that woman was being punished for the sins of a patriarchal society. For one of the points that the novel makes about Lady Dedlock is that, as a scapegoat, she must be far *less* guilty than the society which expurgates its own violence and purifies its shrines by encouraging her death. At some level Dickens *knows* about suppressed sexual violence, and it is this knowledge, working through the dual viewpoint of the two narrators, that provides the impetus for the expulsion of Lady Dedlock when the double narrative is brought together. By implication, it is fear of the destructive power of this violence which reinforces the 'separate spheres' policy of this society and which gives such a fierce edge to the novel's satire of women like Mrs Jellyby, Mrs Pardiggle and Mrs Snagsby, who try to usurp male prerogatives.

In the same way, the dialectic of the dual narrative paradoxically offers both an enactment and a critique of the sexual division into separate spheres. At one level, it enacts it by leading to a conventionally happy ending for the heroine narrator Esther, which comes to her as a reward for proper 'womanly' behaviour. But at another level it deconstructs itself by signally failing to contain the violence it apparently seeks to repress but in fact covertly fosters. The violence, simmering underground throughout the novel, errupts at intervals until it is finally appeased by the cathartic end of Lady Dedlock. Thus Esther's reward can only come at the expense of the destruction of her mother, who takes on all the 'sins' of illicit female sexuality which so threaten the fabric of a patrilineal society. Surely this is what still sticks in the throat about the character of Esther, after all the psychological explanations have been accepted: she is rewarded for having purged her mother's sexual taint, and by so doing, for having connived at what amounts to her own clitoridectomy.

—Virginia Blain, "Double Vision and the Double Standard in *Bleak House:* A Feminist Perspective." Reprinted in *Bleak House*, ed. Jeremy Tambling (New York: St. Martin's Press, 1998): pp. 79–82.

CHRISTINE VAN BOHEEMEN-SAAF ON THE NOVEL AS VICTORIAN FAMILY ROMANCE

[Christine Van Boheemen-Saaf is the author of *Between Sacred and Profane: Narrative Design and the Logic of Myth.* In this essay, she discusses Esther's isolation and repression in the novel.]

Looking back over Esther's development as a character, one notices that the ambivalence of the final symbol of selfhood has been present in Dickens' portrayal of her all along, and reflects an underlying ambivalence in the novel's notion of human identity. From Esther's earliest moments of conscious reflection, her awareness is structured by the tension between her true but unmentionable natural identity and the necessity to ensure a place and role in the patriarchal social system to which she is an outsider. As she gathers from her godmother's unrelenting insistence that she had better not have been born at all, the anniversary of her birth is a day of evil and sinful disgrace to those sharing the secret surrounding her birth. Esther's manner of coping with the social and emotional isolation of her position is to deny that deepest, most natural part of herself, which in her childish understanding merely seems to keep the 'wound' of the day of her birth open. This 'natural' self, on which her own generativity and full womanhood depend, she projects upon her doll, the only one to whom she opens her heart. But this child had better never been born at all: departing for school, Esther buries her doll in the garden. Simultaneously, she sets out to win social approval with the vow 'to repair the fault I had been born with (of which I confessedly felt guilty and yet innocent) . . . and [to] strive as I grew up to be industrious, contented and kind-hearted, and to do some good to some one, and win some love to myself if I could'. From the very beginning, then, Esther's 'self' is split into two halves, one 'buried' and unmentionable, one obsessively concerned with conformity to patriarchal views of feminine identity. We might say that Esther's struggle for selfhood takes place at two levels simultaneously, one questing for an identification with the (m)other in order to achieve sexual identity, the other for substitute fatherhood and a place in society.

Initially, the attempts to earn a place in society and the protection of a father figure occupy the foreground of the narrative. At the Miss

Donnys', and then at Bleak House, Esther persistently attempts to blot out the shame of her birth by trying to become an 'original' herself. As everyone agrees, she is a model of deportment—a 'pattern young lady', as detective Bucket praises her—obsessively creating order out of disorder and stalling the disintegration of society at large (domestically reflected in the state of Mrs Jellyby's closets) by her unrelenting diligence and the protection of her household keys, which she jingles to the refrain of 'Esther, duty, my dear.' Indeed, Esther's attempt to lock out the 'original sin' leads her farther and farther away from selfhood to the perfection of an imaginary, obsessive role, and to speaking to herself in the third person; when her substitute father and guardian finally offers to marry her, it momentarily seems as if Esther will become, like her biblical namesake, 'a queen' of starry purity.

For all Esther's exertions to earn unfallen status, at moments of emotional crisis the repressed image of the doll revives in her memory, bringing with it softer sensations. When the young lawyer Guppy proposes marriage in the chapter entitled 'Signs and Tokens', her own refusal leaves her perturbed: 'I surprised myself by beginning to laugh about it, and then surprised myself still more by beginning to cry about it. . . . I was in a flutter for a little while; and felt as if an old chord had been more coarsely touched than it ever had been since the days of the dear old doll, long buried in the garden.' A similar reaction marks Esther's first meeting with her mother, whom she has never known and who is still a mere stranger to her: 'And, very strangely, there was something quickened within me, associated with the lonely days at my godmother's; yes, away even to the days when I had stood on tiptoe to dress myself at my little glass, after dressing my doll'.

Thus, underneath the narrative strand which moves toward Esther's social rootedness, there is the concern with the buried but stirring insistence of the original 'wound' or 'sin', which must be confronted to be cured or appeased. This confrontation happens, always at the level of implication, in stages. The first begins in the crucially important evening of Esther's contact with Jo, who will transmit the mysterious and highly contagious disease that originates from a rat scurrying from Captain Nemo's pauper grave in Tom-all-Alone's. At that moment, though Esther had not yet learned the identity of her mother—or even of her existence—she has the 'undefinable impression' of 'being something different from what I then was'. As Mark Spilka and Taylor Stoehr have suggested, this disease, never given a name in the novel, is on a symbolic level related to the unbridled sexuality of Esther's parents; and 'smallpox' is indeed close enough to 'pox' to assume a sexual connotation.

In addition, smallpox, a disease which leaves pockmarks on the face, suggests the 'wound' of castration of non-phallic origin. The imagery in which Esther describes the experience of her illness is suggestive of an archetypal and successful quest for identity—she recalls the sensation of crossing a dark lake and of labouring, like a worm, up colossal staircases; however, this confrontation with the uncanny taboo—the return of the repressed—does not lead to the blinding insight of a figure like Oedipus (though it strikes her with temporary blindness). Here is the *anagnorisis* when Esther looks at the pockmarks on her face:

> My hair had not been cut off. . . . It was long and thick. I let it down, and shook it out, and went up to the glass upon the dressing-table. There was a little muslin curtain drawn across it. I drew it back; and stood for a moment looking through such a veil of my own hair, that I could see nothing else. Then I put my hair aside, and looked at the reflection in the mirror. . . . I was very much changed—O very, very much. At first my face was so strange to me, that I think I should have put my hands before it and started back. . . . Very soon it became more familiar, and then I knew the extent of the alteration in it better than I had done at first. It was not like what I had expected; but I had expected nothing definite, and I dare say anything definite would have surprised me.

In this revelation, in which Esther's social self finds her true self fearsomely *unfamiliar,* we recognise the same gesture of moving aside the hair to look at the face which marks the revelatory moment of Esther's later identification of and with her mother. Indeed, the frightening face surrounded by copious hair is an image of the Medusa's head, as Freud has told us, the visual representation of castrated female sexuality that turns the beholder into stone. At one level, then, as a suggestive foreshadowing of the later event, this passage seems to imply Esther's acceptance of the biological truth of her origin without so much as touching the hem of Victorian respectability. However, in the evasiveness of the final phrases, refusing to accept the loss or otherness in denying the existence of a previous expectation, her repression of the reality of her biological self is renewed.

Consequently, her illness results in an increased need to maintain the separateness of the split-off image of the doll rather than its integration. This shows itself in Esther's relationship to Ada Clare, who—like Charley, Esther's little maid—is a reincarnation of the long-buried doll. Charley's wide-eyed tininess suggests the childhood confidante, but Ada has its 'beautiful complexion' and 'rosy lips', and is, moreover, an idealised alter ego: contrary to the sexlessness indicated by Esther's nicknames (Mother Hubbard, Dame Durden, Mrs Shipton), Ada represents feminine sexuality, as indicated by her betrothal to Richard; in contrast to Esther's sense of her own unworthiness, Ada seems bright, beautiful, good, and unblemished. No wonder that Esther seems to love Ada almost more than herself. When Ada marries Richard, Esther hopes to live with them; keeping 'the keys of their house', she will be made 'happy for ever and a day.' When her longing to reconstitute the triangle of family romance in this manner is not fulfilled, Esther is wild with grief. At night she steals to Ada's house and listens to the sounds within! During her illness, it is Ada's pure beauty which must be protected from the disease at all cost. Ada's perfection, the token that she has had no contact with the blight of natural female origin clinging to Esther, is 'the light' in Esther's blindness. During her illness Esther seems to feel that without preserving this idealised version of herself uncontaminated and intact, she cannot continue to live: if Ada is allowed to look upon her marked face for only one moment, Esther will die.

Esther's continued fear of revealing her face to Ada marks her unchanged refusal to accept herself as her mother's daughter. From this point of view, it is highly significant that the chapter that has as its central event the relatively restrained recognition of the kinship between Esther and her mother should end in a climax of much greater emotional intensity with the reunion of Esther and Ada. Here we see Ada play the mother role, accepting Esther's face, 'bathing it with tears and kisses, rocking [her] to and fro like a child, calling [her] by every tender name that she could think of.' Only after Esther has truly accepted the familiarity of her mother's 'sin' will she change positions with Ada: whereas Esther has a romance and starts her own family, the widowed Ada moves back to Bleak House to take care of her guardian.

This moment of acceptance comes after another confrontation with the 'sin' from which all corruption in *Bleak House* has started, after another archetypal descent, which, unlike Esther's illness, is a confrontation with real death. It is the death of Lady Dedlock, who has completed her own circuitous return to the reality of the past and lies dead at the grave of the man 'who should have been her husband', in the spot from which all corruption in the world of his novel takes its origin. This final image of Tom-all-Alone's is the 'primal scene' of the motivation of the narrative. From here the subversive threat of the levelling of hierarchical distinctions—of a breakdown of the walls of subjectivity that ensure the operative power of such concepts as race, class, sex, and age—has arisen, the threat of which the narrator asserts that 'His Grace shall not be able to say Nay to the infamous alliance'. Esther's journey toward this heart of London's darkness, undertaken to 'save' her mother from the final deed, leads her through a 'labyrinth of streets', in between darkness and dawn, into a mental state between waking and dreaming in which the reality she had always known seems so changed that 'great water-gates seemed to be opening and closing in my head, or in the air; and . . . the unreal things were more substantial than the real'. Directly preceding this, she has confessed that it seemed as if the 'stained house-fronts put on human shapes and looked at' her; in the light of the house symbolism of the novel, this seems a hallucinatory realisation that the stain of Tom-all-Alone's is also her own but cannot yet be admitted into consciousness. Thus, when she arrives at the entrance to this enclosed place—the curiously Victorian version of the *hortus conclusus*—she still cannot relate its otherness to herself:

> The gate was closed. Beyond it, was a burial-ground—a dreadful spot in which the night was very slowly stirring; but where I could dimly see . . . houses . . . on whose walls a thick humidity broke out like a disease. On the step at the gate, drenched in the fearful wet of such a place, which oozed and splashed down everywhere, I saw, with a cry of pity and horror, a woman lying—Jenny, the mother of the dead child.

But this last phrase is not final; it is to be revised into the 'dead mother of the living child'. The truth about her own face will come home after a gesture we remember from Esther's illness: 'I lifted the heavy head, put the long dank hair aside, and turned the face. And it was my mother, cold and dead'. At last, then, the unfortunate girl has owned her mother, has looked the evil of her birth in the face and accepted it as her own; from this moment on the taboo on her sexuality is lifted. Avoided the mistakes of her mother, Esther does not marry the elderly Jarndyce, who calls her 'my child', but confesses her hitherto unacknowledged attraction to Alan Woodcourt.

—Christine Van Boheemen-Saaf, "'The Universe Makes an Indifferent Parent': *Bleak House* and the Victorian Family Romance." Reprinted in *Bleak House*, ed. Jeremy Tambling (New York: St. Martin's Press, 1998): pp. 54–59.

HAROLD BLOOM ON THE NOVEL AS CANONICAL

[Harold Bloom, the editor of this collection, is Sterling Professor of the Humanities at Yale University and Henry W. and Albert A. Berg Professor of English at the New York University Graduate School. He is the author of over 20 books and the editor of more than 30 anthologies of literary criticism. His most recent work is the 1998 study *Shakespeare: The Invention of the Human*. In this essay, Bloom discusses Dickens's connection to his character Esther Summerson.]

No nineteenth-century novelist, not even Tolstoy, was stronger than Dickens, whose wealth of invention almost rivals Chaucer and Shakespeare. *Bleak House*, most critics now tend to agree, is his central work; Dickens had enormous affection for *David Copperfield*, but this was his Portrait of the Artist as a Young Man. The Dickens cosmos, his phantasmagoric London and visionary England, emerges in *Bleak House* with a clarity and pungency that surpasses the rest of his work, before and after. No other novel in English invents so much, though perhaps more in the mode of Ben Jonson than of Shakespeare. A Dickens protagonist frequently cannot change and tends to be diminished by action, observations in which I follow G. K. Chesterton, my favorite critic of Dickens, as he is also of Chaucer and of Browning. We do not expect Uriah Heep and

Pecksniff and Squeers to change any more than we could confront mutations of consciousness in Volpone or Sir Epicure Mammon. But Esther Summerson certainly does keep changing; in his subtle creation of her first-person narrative as of her character and personality, Dickens is often underestimated.

I must admit that each time I reread the novel, I tend to cry whenever Esther Summerson cries, and I don't think I am being sentimental. The reader must identify with her or simply not read the book in the old-fashioned sense of reading, which is the only sense that matters. We are, insofar as we are traumatized, versions of Esther; like her, we "recollect forwards." Esther weeps at every mark of kindness and love that she encounters; at our best, when we are not caught in death in life, we are tempted to weep also. Trauma recollects forward; every remission from it brings on tears of relief and joy.

Esther's trauma is universal because it derives from the burden of parentlessness, and sooner or later we are all condemned to be without living parents. Feminist critics have been exercised by the notion that Esther is the victim of a patrilinear society, and they tend not to admire John Jarndyce, much against Dickens's entire art of representation. Dickens, as a great literary artist, is no more patriarchal than Shakespeare, and the creator of Rosalind and Cleopatra does not seem to me ideologically patriarchal. Whatever ideology Shakespeare the man had we do not know. Dickens the husband, father, and prophet of household wisdom certainly was an ideologue of patriarchy, which John Stuart Mill properly resented; but the creator of Esther Summerson, the novelist Dickens, is no ideologue. Esther, who cannot stop deprecating herself, is one of the most intelligent characters in the history of the novel and seems to me a much more authentic portrait of essential elements in Dickens's spirit than David Copperfield ever is. Dickens would never have said what Flaubert said of his relation to Emma Bovary; how odd it would be if he had confessed, "I am Esther Summerson." I suggest, however, that he is.

Esther is the unifying figure in *Bleak House*'s double plot; only she brings together the Kafkan labyrinth of Chancery and the tragedy of her mother, Lady Dedlock. Her link to Chancery is not the fall of Richard Carstone and his marriage to Ada, but rather the negation of Chancery by her guardian John Jarndyce, a negation in which she participates. The prime function of John Jarndyce in *Bleak House* is not that he be the most amiable and ultimately selfless of patriarchs (and he is), but that his absolute dismissal of Chancery be maintained consistently, so as to prove that a labyrinth made by man can be dissolved by man. One of the blessings of Dickens's powerful influence upon Kafka is the altogether Borgesian impact of Kafka upon our understanding of Dickens. Chancery, like the Trial and the Castle in Kafka, is a Gnostic vision: the Law has been usurped by the Cosmocrator, the Demiurge. Blake had no effect upon Dickens, yet *Bleak House* reads like a very Blakean book thanks to a shared Gnostic perspective, though Dickens's heretical impulse is anything but conscious. Chancery in *Bleak House* cannot be reformed; it is burned up only when you cease to behold it, as John Jarndyce and Esther refuse to behold it. That seems to be the apocalyptic meaning of poor Mr. Krook's spontaneous combustion, the most notorious weirdness of *Bleak House* (though there are many others, all to the enhancement of a novel that is also a fantasy-romance). Mad but rather kind, Krook goes up like a bonfire because of his self-admitted symbolic identity with the Lord Chancellor.

Esther Summerson has always divided critics, from Dickens's day until ours; I don't think she has divided common readers, or critics who have remained intuitive readers. *Bleak House*'s rhetorical ironies are mostly crowded into the anonymous narrator's chapters. Dickens excludes overt irony from Esther's narrative until she is strong and healed enough to make her own ironical judgments, as she finally does against Skimpole and others. She seems less Dickens's experiment in representing selflessness or even trauma than she is his one extended attempt, necessarily Shakespearean, at depicting psychological change. In some ways Dickens creates her against the grain of his own genius, as he perhaps realized. Although phantasmagoria overwhelms her in her mysterious illness and its aftermath, she is less of the Dickens world than her parents are, since both Nemo and Lady Dedlock emerge from the characteristic turbulence of Dickensian drives. Esther stands apart, so different from Dickens's flamboyance that he sometimes seems lovingly in awe of her. She is his contribution to the British tradition of heroines of the Protestant will, descended from Clarissa Harlowe and concluding in Lawrence's women in love, Ursula and Gudrun Brangwen; in Forster's sisters, Margaret and Helen in *Howard's End*; and in Woolf's Lily Briscoe in *To the Lighthouse*.

Esther seems less solitary when we contrast her with *Middle-march*'s Dorothea Brooke or with Hardy's Marty South in *The Woodlanders*. A selfless will is very nearly an oxymoron, but Esther is in her way a formidable rhetorician, and her characteristic mode is understatement. She is a survivor, and her mildness is a defense against trauma. Her entire personality is a highly purposeful mechanism for outlasting trauma and resisting the maniac society that attributes guilt to illegitimacy. Although she never wastes energy by fighting back against her society, she never once yields to its obscene moral judgments, even when she is a little girl compelled to endure her godmother's tirades about her perpetual shame. Even the child Esther knows that she is innocent and that her salvation from societal madness depends on her own moral intelligence and her preternatural capacity for patience. Her overt rhetoric of self-deprecation is a powerful defense against not only an abominable system but, more crucially, against her own traumatization, of which she is deeply aware. "Silence, exile, cunning"—the only weapons that Joyce's Stephen would allow himself—Joyce derived not from David Copperfield but from Esther Summerson, who in her oceanic passivity remains the most formidable consciousness in all of Dickens, indeed in all of British literature of the Democratic Age.

Disliking Esther is an easy option for the "materialist" critics of the School of Resentment. Esther is not exactly a feminist ideal or a Marxist exemplar of rebellion. Their heroine in *Bleak House* should be the splendid Hortense, a forerunner of the even more superb Madame DuFarge of *A Tale of Two Cities*, written seven years later. Hortense, like the still fiercer Madame DuFarge, stimulates Dickens's and the reader's masochism but is overmatched by the healthily resistant Inspector Bucket, the most curious of surprising Dickensian visionaries. Expressionistic, impatient, talkative, and murderous, the attractive Hortense is not a surrogate for Lady Dedlock (as feminine critics assert) but a foil for Esther, highlighting her quietude and her Wordsworthian wise passivity.

Is Esther the victim of a patriarchal society? Her trauma is far too individual to ascribe to the greater stigma attached to an illegitimate girl as opposed to a bastard boy. Nor do I consider her stubborn patience a failure in self-esteem. Here again, in a Borgesian way, Kafka aids the interpretation of *Bleak House*, because he is the master of what I would call canonical patience. For Kafka the only sin is impatience, and there is something awesomely Kafkan about Esther Summerson, by which I mean Franz Kafka the person, rather than his characters or his fictive cosmos. Kafka's personal trauma is strikingly parallel to Esther's (and to Kierkegaard's). All three are adept at Kierkegaardian forward recollection. It is almost as though Esther Summerson had awaited, from her birth onward, the appearance of the strong, benign father, John Jarndyce, as compelling a figure as Dickens creates in *Bleak House*, except for Esther herself. Esther essentially being Dickens, or what Walt Whitman would have called Dickens's "real me" or "me myself," John Jarndyce is the idealized father Dickens longed for, rather than his Micawber-like actual father.

In these days, critics of the newer persuasions mutter darkly that Dickens never tells us the source of Jarndyce's clearly substantial income. That is to mistake the nature of *Bleak House* and to forget that it is as much fantasy-romance as social novel. The benign Jarndyce belongs to romance; perhaps little elves labor for him in a happy valley somewhere, minting faery gold. His names for Esther all point toward making her the little old woman, Dame Durden or Cobweb or whoever, of faery tales, and his careful love for her is almost as maternal as paternal. But mixed with this mother-father of romance there is the pathos of wasted life, of a great refusal doubtless allied to Jarndyce's total aversion to the labyrinth of Chancery. Dickens does not intimate what it was that displaced this fountain of benignity into early retirement at Bleak House.

It is worth noting that most of the important figures in *Bleak House* are based upon prototypes: Skimpole notoriously upon the Romantic essayist Leigh Hunt; Boythorn upon the poet Walter Savage Landor; Bucket upon a noted London police inspector; Hortense upon the Belgian murderess Maria Manning, whose public execution both Dickens and Melville attended. Mrs. Jellyby, Miss Flute, poor Jo, and others all have their models, while Esther herself certainly appears to be very like Dickens's favorite sister-in-law, Georgina Hogarth, who ran his household. Sir Leicester Dedlock has been traced to the sixth duke of Devonshire, while Lady Dedlock, like John Jarndyce, is pure invention. Something of Dickens, perhaps whatever does not become part of Esther, finds expression in Jarndyce; but what matters most in Esther's guardian belongs to romance, as Lady Dedlock does altogether. Jarndyce flees from gratitude, not out of any self-destructiveness but because it is not a romance virtue. Lady Dedlock's flight into death is a pure romance narrative, a parabolic punishment of female transgressiveness by a male society. If there is expiation, it is not for having mothered an illegitimate daughter, but for having abandoned the child to others and to much initial lovelessness.

That, again, is closer to romance and has little to do with patriarchal politics. Dickens's largest decision against romance in the novel is when he breaks the pattern of renunciation by having Jarndyce realize that his true responsibility to Esther is paternal. In marrying Woodhouse rather than Jarndyce, Esther is freed of overdetermination: she will not repeat her mother's story. Her trauma is not wholly lifted from her, the haunting continues, and yet we feel that she will never again be persuaded by her own self-negations. It is astonishing how much of her consciousness Dickens is able to make available to us.

—Harold Bloom, *The Western Canon: The Books and School of the Ages* (New York: Harcourt Brace, 1994): pp. 311–316.

☙

LAURA FASICK ON THE DISEASED BODY IN THE NOVEL

[Laura Fasick is the author of *Vessels of Meaning: Women's Bodies, Gender Norms,* and *Class Bias from Richardson to Lawrence.* In this essay, which originally appeared in the 1996 edition of *Dickens Studies Annual,* Fasick expounds upon the moral structure of *Bleak House.*]

In *Bleak House,* the bodilessness of the lady, here Esther, works to shift the locus of discussion from social wrongs to individual moral stature and even becomes a reproach to the poor. Esther, who glides her way through the book without a single physical description, is early established as the practitioner of the personal touch supreme, a benefactress explicitly contrasted with the institutionalized abstractions of Mrs. Jellyby and the blunderbuss tactlessness of Mrs. Pardiggle. Her superiority is clear because, unlike the two other women, she recognizes that "between us and these people there was an iron barrier"; yet at the same time, she is a moral tutor, whispering Christ's words in a grieving mother's ear. Her function in the poor person's household is as arranger and organizer (even to tidying up a dead baby) *and* as religious instructor: she differs from Mrs. Pardiggle only in the sensitivity with which she approaches such responsibilities. But her presence enforces the norm of individual moral culpability. It is possible to sympathize with the bricklayer's tirade against Mrs. Pardiggle in which he implicitly disclaims responsibility for his condition and explicitly blames it on poor living conditions, but Esther's presence enforces the necessity of their behaving properly to *her* (and Ada). From then on, it becomes possible to judge them by their behavior to their benefactors, as when one of the bricklayers goes "out before" the two young women in order to let them pass. Ironically, Esther succeeds partially in effecting the transformation in the family that Mrs. Pardiggle attempts: she is able to make at least the dead child's sister "ashamed" of acting improperly. Yet she does so by her own self-effacement, by the fact that her ministrations, unlike Mrs. Pardiggle's, are difficult to detect with the naked eye.

Jo's story demonstrates even more strongly the importance of moving from the visible to the felt. Jo begins as an exemplum of the slum "product": a hapless repository of disease and suffering too animal-like to be held accountable. His condition is charged explicitly upon society. In George Ford's estimation, he falls below the line at which it is possible to expect self-help; Jo is one of the truly helpless. The novel allows a hint or two that Jo possesses a moral nature: he attempts to be an honest witness at Nemo's inquest, and he is grateful for Nemo's kindness to him. Yet the third-person narrator responsible for most of his story consistently treats him as subhuman: "vermin" generated by the slums from which he comes, Jo ranks below a dog in consciousness. Rather than a full person, he is a "phenomenon," over the description of which the narrator lingers and to which he returns again and again, embellishing with a richness of disgusting detail that contrasts strongly with Esther's invisibility. The reader sees Jo "in uncompromising colours[, f]rom the sole of [his] foot to the crown of [his] head." We are even told to picture him as being "like a growth of fungus or any unwholesome excrescence." Jo can be described in his full physicality precisely because he is almost entirely flesh. As Torsten Pettersson observes of *Oliver Twist*, such reliance on physiological description as characterization brings Dickens close to Zola-esque naturalism. This implicit naturalism in turn introduces deterministic terms that deny characters like Jo the possibility of free will.

This denial of free will, of course, operates in the service of social criticism: even Jo's bestiality is proof of his victimization. Since he is outside the realm of free will that might make him at least partially responsible for his own condition, society must bear the full blame for what he is. Once Jo enters Esther's narrative and Esther's presence, however, both he and the slum-bred disease he carries undergo a shift in meaning for Esther's narrative assumes both the power of the individual will and the providential ordering of the world.

Disease up to this point in the novel has been primarily a marker of social wrong: disease among indigents is a disgusting extension and visualization of general slum conditions. As such, it is a vehicle of social protest and a proof that society requires drastic revision. But when disease reaches Esther (and even before her, Charley) it is transfigured into an individual moral test and, overwhelmingly, a demonstration of individual moral worth. With the exception of Skimpole, that parasitic invader of other people's homes, everyone connected with Bleak House rises to the occasion, from Charley to Ada to Mr. Jarndyce to Mr. Boythorn and even to the servants. Esther's bodily weakness, in particular, becomes a way to demonstrate the goodness of those around her, and she is even grateful for the opportunity that sends her this demonstration of people's kindness and their love for her. From furnishing an indictment of the larger society of institutions, disease moves to demonstrating the essential health and worthiness of the smaller society of individuals.

The effect is to establish the middle-class home as the site not only of more physical comfort, but of more spiritual potential, than the slum. The pains produced by poverty are degrading morally as well as physical, but illness in the middle-class home reveals angelic spirits. There is therefore a purpose to this suffering—indeed, more than one purpose: it provides examples of nobility for others to follow, gives scope for people's goodness, and reinforces bonds of affection. Esther, Charley's nurse during the latter's illness, records that "[s]o patient she was, so uncomplaining, and inspired by such a gentle fortitude, that very often as I sat by Charley . . . I silently prayed to our Father in heaven that I might not forget the lesson which this little sister taught me." But Charley's virtues during her own sickness are only a prelude to her heroism during Esther's. At that time, she is so deft an attendant that Esther muses she was "sent into the world, surely, to minister to the weak and sick." Esther can find equal utility even in her own pain: her "trivial suffering and change" are "worth" being able "to fill . . . a place" in her guardian's heart. All this commentary discovers a meaning, even a positive value, in what could easily seem merely unwarranted misfortune.

Nor is Esther's commentary, shaped as it is by Esther's resolutely hopeful perspective, the only means whereby disease shifts its meaning. It is significant that Charley is able to retain her "gentle qualities" through all the various times . . . in [her] illness." Suffering here lacks the power that Elaine Scarry ascribes it: it cannot make the sufferer's "created world of thought and feeling, all the psychological and mental content that constitutes both one's self and one's world . . . ceas[e] to exist." Above all, it cannot affect the sufferer's will and free choice. Both Charley and Esther remain exemplary moral agents, despite extreme pain and delirium. Indeed, even Esther's feverish delusions provide another illustration of her conscientious nature: reliving each stage of her life simultaneously, she "was not only oppressed by cares and difficulties adapted to each station, but by the great perplexity of endlessly trying to reconcile them." Wishing only to do right, Esther speaks even of her own mortality as though it were an instrument that she could employ as part of her care-taking role. Warning Charley to keep Ada from her sickroom, Esther declares, "' If you let her in but once, only to look upon me for one moment as I lie here, I shall die.'" Here the death of the body is no more than the means for the soul to express its protective love.

—Laura Fasick, "Dickens and the Diseased Body in *Bleak House*," *Dickens Studies Annual* 24 (1996): pp. 138–141.

Plot Summary of
David Copperfield

David Copperfield is born at Blunderstone Rookery, six months after his father's death (**chapter one**). His father's aunt, Miss Trotwood, arrives on the day of the birth, the first time she has visited since the marriage of her favorite nephew to David's mother, the "wax doll" girl half her nephew's age. "I intend to be her godmother," she says, "and I beg you'll call her Betsey Trotwood Copperfield." The baby is, of course, a boy. She leaves, never to return.

In **chapter two** Mr. Murdstone, a gentleman (whom both David and Peggotty dislike instantly) courts David's mother. David is sent away with Peggotty to Yarmouth while Murdstone and Clara Copperfield marry. At Yarmouth (**chapter three**) David is delighted by the sea town, the sailors, and Peggotty's extended family, some of whom are the orphans of "drowndead" sailors. Ham, Mr. Peggotty's orphaned nephew, will become the focus of one of the novel's tragedies. Of Little Em'ly, the mature David reflects that it may have been better if she had perished in one of her daring displays of fearlessness toward the sea.

David returns home and discovers that Murdstone has become his stepfather. The man dominates his mother and attempts to dominate David. The adult narrator reflects that "A word of encouragement and explanation, of pity for my childish ignorance, of welcome home, or reassurance to me that it was home, might have made me dutiful to him in my heart henceforth, instead of in my hypocritical outside, and might have made me respect instead of hate him." When Miss Murdstone, his stepfather's sister, takes over housekeeping the tyranny over David and his mother is complete.

David is sent away to a school, Salem House, near London (**chapter five**). The heads of the school are told by Murdstone that David's "teeth are to be filed" (**chapter six**). The next day Mr. Creakle advises his assembled pupils, "Take care of what you're about, in this new half. Come fresh up to the lessons, I advise you, for I come fresh up to the punishment. I won't flinch" (**chapter seven**). David recalls that "there never can have been a man who enjoyed his profession more than Mr. Creakle did. He had a delight in cutting at the boys which was like the satisfaction of a craving appetite." James Steerforth, good-looking, condescending, is a privileged, wealthy pupil who promises to take David under his wing. David is oblivious to his inherently bad character; impressed only by his self-confidence and charisma.

On his tenth birthday (**chapter nine**) David receives presents sent from Peggotty and the news from Mr. Creakle that his mother is dead. The baby she had born with Murdstone died soon after. David reflects, "The mother who lay in the grave, was the mother of my infancy; the little creature in her arms, was myself, as I had once been hushed forever on her bosom."

After the funeral Peggotty is fired and David is ignored by the Murdstones (**chapter ten**). He visits Peggotty at Yarmouth and is pleased to see Little Em'ly again. To his surprise, David finds that he is not to return to school. Instead, he will go London to be employed as a laborer, for room and board, at the firm of Murdstone and Grinby (**chapter eleven**). "No words can express the secret agony of my soul as I sunk into this companionship," he recalls, ". . . and I felt my hopes of growing up to be a learned and distinguished man crushed in my bosom."

David boards with the family of Mr. Micawber, a profligate for whom David makes frequent trips to the pawn. Nonetheless, he likes the Micawbers for their optimism no matter the circumstances. Eventually, David visits them in debtors' prison (as Dickens did his own father).

In **chapter twelve** the Micawbers are released from prison. David is saddened by news that they will move to the country and he will again be friendless. David decides to seek out his great-aunt Betsey Trotwood. When all his possession are stolen, he sets out with only the clothes on his back and a few coins. At the home of his aunt (**chapters thirteen** and **fourteen**) she meets with Murdstone to discuss David's future. Murdstone pronounces David "a sullen, rebellious spirit, a violent temper, and an untoward, intractable disposition." Betsey declares that she will assume responsibility for David, and that Murdstone and his sister are no longer welcome. "An thus I began a new life, in a new name, and with everything new about me," observes the narrator.

Soon after, Aunt Betsey tells David, whose name has been shortened to "Trot," that he will go to school in nearby Canterbury (**chapter fifteen**). She takes David with her to visit her lawyer, Mr. Wickfield, to settle matters about the school. Here he meets fifteen-year-old Uriah Heep, a cadaverous boy "stealthily staring at him with sleepless eyes . . . like two red suns." It is decided that David will board with the Wickfields. Aunt Betsey leaves him with advice to "Never be mean in anythin;

never be false, never be cruel." Wickfield's daughter, Agnes, will become David's second wife—and Uriah Heep his enemy because of it.

Of Doctor Strong's school at Canterbury (**chapter sixteen**), David observes that it "was an excellent school; as different from Mr. Creakle's as good is from evil." At home with the Wickfields Uriah Heep studies law and David develops an affection for Agnes.

By **chapter nineteen** David's schooling is finished and he must choose a profession. Aunt Betsey suggests that he try life on his own for awhile; that he visit his friends in London and Yarmouth.

In London he meets Steerforth, now an Oxford student, who promises to make David more sophisticated. David invites him to accompany him to Yarmouth and is puzzled by Steerforth's class snobbery toward the Peggottys. They arrive at the Peggottys just as Little Em'ly's engagement to Ham is announced. Steerforth confides to David that Ham is "too chuckleheaded" for her. In **chapter twenty-two** we realize that Em'ly has begun a secret affair with Steerforth.

David decides, at the suggestion of his aunt, that he will choose the law as his profession (**chapter twenty-three**). She is happy to pay the fee for his training, asking only that he "be a loving child to me in my age, and bear with my whims and fancies." On their way to the law firm his aunt is disturbed by a man David thinks is a beggar. Aunt Betsey drives him away, but not before she has given him a considerable amount of cash. The man is, in fact, her long-lost husband who is now blackmailing her.

Steerforth leads David from his "first dissipation" in drinking and theatre-going to the shocking realization that he has seduced Em'ly (**chapters twenty-four** through **thirty-one**). David feels responsible, since it was he who introduced Steerforth to Em'ly. He now considers Steerforth "a cherished friend, who [is] dead." David observes that, among the neighborhood, "Many were hard on her, some few were hard upon him" (**chapter thirty-two**). Mrs. Steerforth is aghast that her son should have disgraced her by marrying low.

David's thoughts turn to his infatuation with Dora Spenlow, the daughter of his employer (**chapter twenty-six**). By **chapter thirty-three** they are engaged, and David is convinced that "[t]he greater the accumulation of deceit and trouble in the world, the brighter and purer shone the star of Dora high above the world." In **chapter thirty-four**, another shift in David's fortunes occurs. The money he had been able to rely upon after his mother's death is now gone. He must take care of himself.

By **chapter thirty-five** David fears poverty. His aunt has no money; she moves in with David. David tries, without success, to get back at least part of the fee his aunt paid for his law apprenticeship. He is surprised one day to see Agnes Wickfield in a passing carriage. She is in London with her father and Uriah Heep, now her father's law partner. Agnes suggests that David apply for a job as secretary to his old Canterbury master, Dr. Strong.

David is entusiastic about his prospects (**chapter thirty-six**), determined to prove to his aunt that her confidence in him is well-placed—and to win Dora. The job and the pay are modest, but David gladly accepts. He writes to Dora, who knows nothing of his new poverty, and asks if she could love such a beggar. She cannot believe he is serious. He suggests that she learn housekeeping skills; he promises to send her a cookbook and she faints.

In **chapter thirty-eight** David studies shorthand in preparation to become a Parliamentary reporter, determined to gain Dora's confidence. Mr. Spenlow advises him that marriage to his daughter is impossible, and David is left utterly despairing. The next morning, he is told the astonishing news that Mr. Spenlow had died the day before. Ironically, he has left Dora nearly penniliess, and she is sent to live with her two maiden aunts. Dora, still incompetent but very beautiful, agrees to marry David.

Dora and Agnes meet, in **chapter forty-two**, and the contrast in their characters prepares the reader for David's eventual marriage to Agnes. The women like each other instantly. Dora remarks to David, "Don't you think, if I had had her for a friend a long time ago, . . . I might have been more clever perhaps? . . . I wonder why you ever fell in love with me?" Agnes encourages their relationship, "I can be happier in nothing than in your happiness," she tells him.

David is now twenty-one and a respected newspaper reporter (**chapter forty-three**). His income has made it possible for his aunt to move into a cottage of her own and for him to marry Dora, at last. After the honeymoon, David observes that "All the romance of our engagement [was] put away upon a shelf to rust—no one to please but one another—one another to please, for life. . . . I doubt whether two young girds could have known less about keeping house, then I and my pretty Dora did." The household is an ill-managed disaster. As his reputation grows,

David spends more time writing—and Dora sits beside him, holding his pens.

In **chapter forty-six**, a year has passed, and David has grown more successful. He learns that Em'ly, abandoned by Steerforth in Italy, has disappeared. David visits Mr. Peggotty to tell him this news, and they decide that Em'ly would come to London. In **chapters fifty** and **fifty-one** Mr. Peggotty and David find Em'ly and now, happily reunited with those who love her, she agrees to emigrate with her uncle to Australia.

In **chapter forty-eight** David has published a book and given up Parliamentary reporting to be an author full-time. He and Dora no longer squabble about housekeeping. Sometimes he thinks about his contentment with Agnes and wonders what would have happened if he had not met Dora. Their child dies at birth and Dora never recovers her health. In **chapter fifty-three**, both know she is dying, and Dora asks David to send for Agnes. Dora tells David she knows she was not a suitable wife for him: "I was too young. I don't mean in years only, but in experience, and thoughts, and everything." "It is much better as it is," she tells him. She asks him to send Agnes to her. When Agnes returns, Dora—and her little dog, sleeping at David's feet—are dead.

Chapter fifty-five marks a cruel turn of events. Ham has had David write to Em'ly on his behalf to profess his continued love. When he receives no answer, he decides to confront her before she sails. Before this can happen, there is a shipwreck near the coast at Yarmouth and Ham swims out, with a rope tied around his waist, in an attempt to save the lone survivor clinging to the mast. Ham drowns, and later the body of the man Ham tried to save is washed ashore. It is James Steerforth. As the emigrants prepare to set sail for Australia (**chapter fifty-seven**) David tells Micawber to intercept all news of the drowning to keep it from Mr. Peggotty and Em'ly.

David, too, leaves England (**chapter fifty-eight**) to wander, mourning for his "child-wife, taken from her blooming world, so young," and for his friend, Ham. He spends time in Switzerland, where he writes his third novel, returning home after three years. It occurs to him that he is in love with Agnes, that Agnes is the right wife for him.

After they are quietly married (**chapter sixty-two**), Agnes tells David of Dora's last request, that they should marry. As David finishes his narrative, looking back upon his long life, he thinks of Agnes, whose "face shines on him like a heavenly light." ❀

List of Characters in
David Copperfield

David Copperfield is the protagonist and narrator of the novel. He recalls in maturity a childhood beset by all the social injustice and corruption Dickens meant to expose. The trials and abuses David suffers are more psychic than physical, beginning with the trouncing of his affectionate nature by his mother's new husband, Mr. Murdstone. His story centers around two great tests of his character: In the first, after the death of his mother, he is denied education and fears "growing up to be a shabby, moody man, lounging an idle life away. . . ." In the second, after his Aunt Betsey loses her fortune, he must become entirely self-reliant. He becomes a successful writer. But David always needs someone's support, and when he marries Dora, his disappointment centers on her inability to help him. His second marriage is more successful.

Betsey Trotwood is David's paternal great aunt. She arrives on the day of his birth, only to leave abruptly when she discovers that the newborn is not a girl. David turns to her after his mother's death; she finances his education and becomes like a mother to him.

Clara Peggotty is his mother's housekeeper and David's nurse—until she is fired by the Murdstones after the marriage of David's mother to Edward Murdstone. After his mother's death she becomes like a mother to him.

Ham Peggotty is the orphaned nephew of Daniel Peggotty. He is a kindly, quiet man who becomes a fisherman and boat builder. Shortly after their engagement, Little Em'ly deserts him. He drowns trying to save her seducer.

Little Em'ly is the orphaned niece of Daniel Peggotty. She is pretty and intelligent, but wishes more than anything to rise above her social strata. Steerforth is able to seduce her away from Ham Peggotty by promising to make her a "lady." She later emigrates to Australia with her uncle.

James Steerforth is David's school friend at Salem House. Handsome and egotistical, he leads David toward a dissipated life. He seduces Em'ly, then abandons her. Ham Peggotty attempts to rescue him from a shipwreck; both drown.

Wilkins Micawber is optimistic, good-hearted, and thoroughly profligate. He is one of the great comic figures in English fiction. David lives with the Micawbers after leaving school to work in the warehouse. Micawber becomes clerk to Uriah Heep. He eventually emigrates to Australia, where he becomes a magistrate.

Emma Micawber is the wife of Wilkins Micawber, and the mother of numerous children. Much like her husband in temperament, she has faith in his abilities and trusts his judgment.

Uriah Heep is a clerk in Mr. Wickfield's law firm and one of Dickens's most striking grotesques. Having attended a charity school, he hates and envies the upper classes. Plotting and scheming to achieve his goals, he manipulates Wickfield and nearly forces Agnes to marry him. Exposed as a forger, he later is found serving a life sentence in prison.

Mr. Wickfield is Betsey Trotwood's lawyer (solicitor) and Agnes's father.

Dora Spenlow is David's first wife. She is the daughter of his employer. Pampered as a child and brought up in luxury, Dora has neither the skills nor the interest to manage household concerns. Her haplessness is a burden on David as a struggling young writer. Her death makes possible David's marriage to Agnes.

Agnes Wickfield is David's second wife, and the daughter of Mr. Wickfield, Aunt Betsey's lawyer. Unlike Dora, Agnes is not accustomed to luxury and has formidable domestic talents. Her father proudly refers to her as his "little housekeeper." Dora, on her death bed, tells Agnes to marry David. At the close of the book he imagines her "face shining on him like a heavenly light." ❀

Critical Views on
David Copperfield

CHARLES DICKENS ON THE NOVEL

[In this extract, from Dickens's introduction to the first edition of *David Copperfield*, the author calls the book his favorite.]

⟨ . . . ⟩ I did not find it easy to get sufficiently far away from it, in the first sensations of having finished it, to refer to it with the composure which this formal heading would seem to require. My interest in it was so recent and strong, and my mind was so divided between pleasure and regret—pleasure in the achievement of a long design, regret in the separation from many companions—that I was in danger of wearying the reader with personal confidences and private emotions.

Besides which, all that I could have said of the Story to any purpose, I had endeavoured to say in it.

It would concern the reader little, perhaps, to know how sorrowfully the pen is laid down at the close of a two-years' imaginative task; or how an Author feels as if he were dismissing some portion of himself into the shadowy world, when a crowd of the creatures of his brain are going from him for ever. Yet, I had nothing else to tell; unless, indeed, I were to confess (which might be of less moment still), that no one can ever believe this Narrative in the reading more than I believed it in the writing.

So true are these avowals at the present day, that I can now only take the reader into one confidence more. Of all my books, I like this the best. It will be easily believed that I am a fond parent to every child of my fancy, and that no one can ever love that family as dearly as I love them. But, like many fond parents, I have in my heart of hearts a favourite child. And his name is David Copperfield.

—Charles Dickens, "Preface" to *David Copperfield*, 1850.

[Mowbray Morris (1847–1911) was a British writer and critic. He is the author of the novels *Tales of the Spanish Main, Montrose,* and *Claverhouse,* the critical volumes *Charles Dickens* and *Essays on Theatrical Criticism,* and editor of *Boswell's Life of Johnson.* In this extract, he discusses the strength of the characters in *David Copperfield,* and confirms the author's belief that this novel is his best work.]

I have said that in *David Copperfield* Dickens is freer from defect than in any other of his works. It is rarely that public opinion has ratified an author's judgment so completely as it has here. As we all know, this was Dickens's favourite, and the reason we all know. It may be noted in passing how characteristic of the two men is their choice. To Dickens *David Copperfield* was, to use his own words, his favourite child, because in its pages he saw the reflection of his own youth. Thackeray, though he never spoke out on such matters, is generally believed to have looked not a little into his own heart when he wrote *Pendennis.* Yet his favourite was *Esmond,* for *Esmond* he rightly felt to be the most complete and perfect of his works; in that exquisite book his *art* touched its highest point. With *David Copperfield,* no doubt the secret of the writer's partiality is in some sense the secret of the reader's. Though none, perhaps, have been so outspoken as Hogg, every man takes pleasure in writing about himself, and we are always pleased to hear what he has to say; egotism, as Macaulay says, so unpopular in conversation, is always popular in writing. But not in the charm of autobiography alone lies the fascination which this delightful book has exercised on every class of readers. It is not only Dickens's most attractive work, but it is his best work. And it is his best for this reason, that whereas in all his others he is continually striving to realise the conception of his fancy, in this alone his business is to idealise the reality; in this alone, as it seems to me, his imagination prevails over his fancy. In this alone he is never grotesque, or for him so rarely that we hardly care to qualify the adverb. Nowhere else is his pathos so tender and so sure; nowhere else is his humour, though often more boisterous and more abundant, so easy and so fine; nowhere else is his observation so vivid and so deep; nowhere else has he held with so sure a hand the balance between the classes. If in the character of Daniel Peggotty more eloquently and more reasonably than he has ever done elsewhere, even in honest Joe Gargery, he has enlarged on his favourite abiding-place for virtue, he has also nowhere else been so ready and so glad to welcome her in those more seemly places wherein for the most part he can find no resting-place for her feet. Weak-minded as Doctor Strong is, fatuous, if the reader pleases, we are never asked to laugh at the kindly, chivalrous old scholar, as we are at Sir Leicester Dedlock; Clara Pegotty is no better woman than Agnes Wickfield. And even in smaller matters, and in the characters of second-rate importance, we may find the same sureness of touch. It has been made a reproach against him that his characters are too apt to be forgotten in the externals of their callings, that they never speak without some allusion to their occupations, and cannot be separated from them. In the extraordinary number and variety of characters that he has drawn, no doubt one can find instances of this. For so many of these characters, nearly all, indeed, of the comic ones, real as he has made them to us, are not, when we come to examine them, realities, but rather conceptions of his fancy, which he has to shape into realities by the use of certain traits and peculiarities of humanity with which his extraordinary observation has supplied him. Major Pendennis, and Costigan, and Becky Sharp *are* realities whom Thackeray idealises, makes characters of fiction out of. But Sam Weller and Mrs. Gamp are the children of fancy whom Dickens makes real, partly by the addition of sundry human attributes, but even more so by the marvelous skill and distinctness with which he brings them and keeps them before us. But in order to do this he is obliged never to lose sight, or to suffer us to lose sight, of those peculiarities, whether of speech, or manner, or condition, which make them for us the realities that they are. And in so doing it cannot but happen that he seems to thrust those peculiarities at times somewhat too persistently upon us. In *David Copperfield* this is not so, or much less so than anywhere else, except, of course, in *The Tale of Two Cities*, Dickens's only essay at the romance proper, where the characters are subordinate to the story. We may see this, for example, by comparing Omer, the undertaker, in *David Copperfield*, with Mould, the undertaker, in *Martin Chuzzlewit*. Mould and all his family live in a perpetual atmosphere of funerals; his children are represented as solacing their young existences by "playing at buryin's down in the shop, and follerin' the order-book to its long home in the iron safe;" and Mr. Mould's own idea of fellowship is of a person "one would almost feel disposed to bury for nothing, and do it neatly, too!" On his first introduction, after old Anthony's death, he sets the seal on his personality by the remark that Jonas's liberal orders for the funeral prove "what was so forcibly observed by the lamented theatrical poet—*buried at Stratford*—that there is good in everything." That touch is very comical, but also very grotesque; it is a touch of fancy, not of nature. But when David Copperfield, as a man, recalls himself to the recollection of the good-hearted Omer, who had known him as a boy, the undertaker is revealed in a very different fashion. "To be sure," said Mr. Omer, touching my waistcoat with his forefinger; "and there was a little child too! *There was two parties. The little party was laid along with the other party.* Over at Blunderstone it was, of course. Dear me! And how have you been since?" Every one must be conscious of the difference here.

—Mowbray Morris, "Charles Dickens," *Fortnightly Review* (Dec. 1882): pp. 776–777.

⟨᭡⟩

WILLIAM SAMUEL LILLY ON THE SOBER VERACITY OF THE NOVEL

[In this essay, William Samuel Lilly takes a different view of *David Copperfield* from the author and Mowbray Morris. Here, he argues that the novel is far from a masterpiece, although he does note that *David Copperfield* is the best of Dickens's works.]

There is much—very much—⟨in *David Copperfield*⟩ which we could wish away. In fact I, if I take the book up, give effect to my wish, and practically put aside a great deal of it. And no doubt many other readers do the same. But it is informed by a simple power, a sober veracity, a sustained interest, peculiarly its own among its author's works. Dickens's young men are, as a rule, impossible. They are well-nigh all of the same inane type. He seems to have got them out of an Adelphi melodrama. But David Copperfield, who is a transcript from his own troublous and distressed childhood and youth, is, at all events, human. His young women are as inane as his young men. His amatory scenes—good heavens let us not speak of them and their mawkish sentimentalities! What a theme for a poet had he in Steerforth and Little Em'ly! How George Sand would have treated it! How George Eliot has treated a similar theme in *Adam Bede!* But Dickens possessed no words to tell forth that idyll. And if he had possessed them he dared not to have uttered them. He stood in too much awe of Mr. Podsnap's "young person." The history of the love of Steerforth and Little Em'ly was impossible to him. He could not have narrated it if he would; and he would not if he could.

I think he never again wrote so felicitously as in *David Copperfield.* No doubt he did many fine things afterwards in the way of genre painting. We may regard him as a literary Teniers. But as years went on his manner seems to me to grow more unnatural, more stilted, more intolerable. The higher art which he tried to grasp, ever eluded him. There is an absence of composition in his work; there is no play of light and shade; there is no proportion, no perspective. His books cannot be said to be composed, they are improvised.

—William Samuel Lilly, *Four English Humourists of the Nineteenth Century* (1895). Reprinted in *The New Moulton Library,* ed. Harold Bloom (New York: Chelsea House Publishers, 1989): p. 4887.

⊗

ALGERNON CHARLES SWINBURNE ON THE NOVEL AS MASTERPIECE

[Algernon Charles Swinburne (1837–1909) was an important English poet and critic. His works include the drama *Atalanta in Calydon* (1865), three plays on Mary, Queen of Scots, and criticism of William Blake and the Brontë sisters, in addition to Dickens. In this essay, Swinburne compares *David Copperfield* to Dickens's earlier works, and calls the novel a "masterpiece."]

David Copperfield, from the first chapter to the last, is unmistakable by any eye above the level and beyond the insight of a beetle's as one of the masterpieces to which time can only add a new charm and an unimaginable value. The narrative is as coherent and harmonious as that of *Tom Jones;* and to say this is to try it by the very highest and apparently the most unattainable standard. But I must venture to reaffirm my conviction that even the glorious masterpiece of Fielding's radiant and beneficent genius, if in some points superior, is by no means superior in all. Tom is a far completer and more living type of gallant boyhood and generous young manhood than David; but even the lustre of Partridge is palid and lunar beside the noontide glory of Micawber. Blifil is a more poisonously plausible villain than Uriah: Sophia Western remains unequalled except by her sister heroine Amelia as a perfectly credible and adorable type of young English womanhood, naturally 'like one of Shakespeare's women,' socially as fine and true a lady as Congreve's Millamant or Angelica. But even so large-minded and liberal a genius as Fielding's could never have conceived any figure like Miss Trotwood's any group like that of the Peggottys. As easily could it have imagined and realised the magnificent setting of the story, with its homely foreground of street or wayside and its background of tragic sea.

The perfect excellence of this masterpiece has perhaps done some undeserved injury to the less impeccable works of genius which immediately succeeded it. But in *Bleak House* the daring experiment of combination or alteration which divides a story between narrative in the third person and narrative in the first is justified and vindicated by its singular and fascinating success. 'Esther's narrative' is as good as her creator's; and no enthusiasm of praise could overrate the excellence of them both. For wealth and variety of character none of the master's works can be said to surpass and few can be said to equal it. When all necessary allowance has been made for occasional unlikeliness in detail or questionable methods of exposition, the sustained interest and the terrible pathos of Lady Dedlock's tragedy will remain unaffected and unimpaired. Any reader can object that a lady visiting a slum in the disguise of a servant would not have kept jewelled rings on her fingers for the inspection of a crossing-sweeper, or that a less decorous and plausible way of acquainting her with the fact that a scandalous episode in her early life was no longer a secret for the family lawyer could hardly have been imagined than the public narrative of her story in her own drawing-room by way of an evening's entertainment for her husband and their guest. To these objections, which any Helot of culture whose brain may have been affected by habitual indulgence in the academic delirium of self-complacent superiority may advance or may suggest with the most exquisite infinity of impertinence, it may be impossible to retort an equally obvious and inconsiderable objection.

But to a far more serious charge, which even now appears to survive the confutation of all serious evidence, it is incomprehensible
and inexplicable that Dickens should have returned no better an
answer than he did. Harold Skimpole was said to be Leigh Hunt; a
rascal after the order of Wainewright, without the poisoner's comparatively and diabolically admirable audacity of frank and fiendish
self-esteem, was assumed to be meant for a portrait or a caricature
of an honest man and a man of unquestionable genius. To this most
serious and most disgraceful charge Dickens merely replied that he
never anticipated the identification of the rascal Skimpole with the
fascinating Harold—the attribution of imaginary villainy to the
original model who suggested or supplied a likeness for the externally amiable and ineffectually accomplished lounger and shuffler
through life. The simple and final reply should have been that indolence was the essential quality of the character and conduct and philosophy of Skimpole—'a perfectly idle man: a mere amateur,' as he
describes himself to the sympathetic and approving Sir Leicester;
that Leigh Hunt was one of the hardest and steadiest workers on
record, throughout a long and chequered life, at the toilsome trade
of letters; and therefore that to represent him as a heartless and
shameless idler would have been about as rational an enterprise, as
lifelike a design after the life, as it would have been to represent Shelley
as a gluttonous and canting hypocrite or Byron as a loyal and unselfish
friend. And no one as yet, I believe, has pretended to recognize in Mr.
Jarndyce a study from Byron, in Mr. Chadband a libel on Shelley.

—Algernon Charles Swinburne, "Charles Dickens," *Quarterly Review*
(July 1902). Reprinted in *The New Moulton Library*, ed. Harold
Bloom (New York: Chelsea House Publishers, 1989): p. 4905.

❦

STANLEY FRIEDMAN ON THE MODEL FOR URIAH HEEP

[In this essay, Stanley Friedman claims that Dickens's model
for Uriah Heep was a former friend, Thomas Powell.
Friedman discusses how the relationship between Dickens and
Powell deteriorated, and shows how this was written into the
author's autobiographical masterpiece, *David Copperfield.*]

Late in *David Copperfield* Mr Micawber stridently tells David, Traddles, Aunt Betsey, and Mr Dick of Uriah Heep's criminal behaviour:

> Villany is the matter; baseness is the matter; deception, fraud, conspiracy, are the matter; and the name of the whole atrocious mass is—HEEP!

Continuing the tirade, Micawber employs epithets like 'the abandoned rascal', 'interminable cheat, and liar', and 'consummate scoundrel'. Subsequently, in the great comic exposure scene, he confronts and angrily excoriates Uriah: 'a scoundrel', 'probably the most consummate Villain that has ever existed', 'the Forger and the Cheat'.

These intemperate exclamations appear in Nos 16 and 17 of the novel, the instalments for August and September 1850, written respectively during July and August 1850. Strangely, however, approximately seven to ten months before composing these remarks for Micawber, Dickens himself had used extremely similar language in letters vigorously attacking a man with whom he had once been on amicable terms, Thomas Powell: 'the villainy and unblushing falsehood of that execrable rascal Powell', 'such an unmitigated villain', 'a Forger and a Thief'. 'this unutterable scoundrel', 'this most consummate Villain'.

Of all the commentators on *David Copperfield*, only one, I believe, has proposed a link between Powell and Heep; and this writer, Peter Ackroyd, offers merely the following statement:

> ... there was anger and resentment in Dickens during this period [December 1849], particularly against Thomas Powell. Certainly it is possible that the memory of the experience of these feelings was one he used to direct David Copperfield's hostility against Uriah Heep in the chapter he was then writing.

But Ackroyd here refers to Chapter 25, in No 9, composed in December 1849, not Chapters 49 and 52, in which Micawber's diatribes appear. Moreover, the part played by Powell in the development of Heep may go beyond the hostility felt by David and Dickens, since various misdeeds of Uriah's, as well as his eventual departure from England are possibly derived from Powell's career. Even though the presentation of Heep before No 9 was evidently not based on Powell, Uriah as he appears in the remainder of the story may provide another case in which Dickens found inspiration in a live model. Indeed, the novelist perhaps came to see his creation of Uriah as a way of getting a measure of covert revenge against Powell, a man who had suddenly revealed himself as a malicious, unscrupulous, and defamatory enemy. Just as the child David, when reading the great books left by his father, 'consoled' himself 'by impersonating' his 'favorite characters in them' and 'by putting Mr. and Miss Murdstone into all the bad ones', so Dickens, in writing rather than in reading, may have cast his foe Thomas Powell into the role of the despicable Uriah Heep.

Although we cannot be certain when Dickens first met Powell, one source reports that the two were included in a group taken by Powell's employer, the wealthy London merchant Thomas Chapman, to see restored Crosby Hall on July 27, 1842. The friendly relationship that developed between the novelist and Powell, who was nearly two and a half years older and aspired to recognition as a poet and dramatist, can be traced in the extant correspondence that the latter received from Dickens. The first preserved letter, written on October 9, 1843, conveys thanks for an 'elegant present' and then offers banter in a facetious tone suggesting cordial relations between writer and recipient. In the next surviving piece (February 24, 1844), a brief note, Dickens introduces his seventeen-year-old brother, Augustus, whom the merchant Chapman had agreed to employ. The whimsical opening, 'I enclose the brother, concerning whom Mr Chapman has been so kind as to talk with you,' implies that Powell, Chapman's managing clerk, had been asked to train and supervise the young man.

Writing to Powell again on March 2, 1844, Dickens begins, 'I really am more indebted and obliged to you that I can express, for your great interest and kindness in the matter of my small "bit of blood"' (a reference to Augustus), and concludes with a warm invitation to dinner: 'I shall be delighted to see you.' Some weeks later, on April 16, 1844, Dickens sent a letter still friendlier and even more familiar in its jesting tone, including another invitation to dinner. After this, the letters that have been preserved are all very short and unrevealing, with one important exception. On August 2, 1845, a letter is evidently in response to Powell's expression of concern over a romantic attachment between Augustus and an unidentified young lady. After deferentially stating, 'I . . . am disposed (subject always to your corrective judgment) to leave the matter where it is'—that is, to avoid interfering, Dickens maintains that the attachment in question seems to pose no real threat, and he then confidingly describes his own youthful experience of love:

> . . . once I really set upon the cast for six or seven long years, all the energy and determination of which I am owner. But it went the way of nearly all such things at last, though I think it kept me steadier than the working of my nature was, to many good things for the time. If anyone had interfered with my very small Cupid, I don't know what absurdity I might not have committed in assertion of his proper liberty; but having plenty of rope he hanged himself, beyond all chance of restoration.

Dickens's willingness to describe his own frustrating courtship of Maria Beadnell and his earlier openness in discussing his brother's personal life suggest a trusting relationship with Powell. Although this friendship seems to have developed beyond its initial stages largely because of the older man's assistance to young Augustus, the surviving letters suggest some degree of compatability and closeness between Dickens and Powell.

In the summer of 1846, however, after Dickens and Powell had been on friendly terms for at least some two and a half years, Thomas Chapman, the employer of Powell, discovered that this man had stolen £10,000, an extremely large sum, through forgery and embezzlement. On July 3, 1846, Dickens replied to a letter from Chapman:

> I have been perfectly horrified by the whole Story. I could hardly name a man in London whom I should have thought less likely to stand so committed, than he. Not that I had any intimate knowledge of his pursuits, or any close acquaintance with himself or his usual mode of thinking and proceeding—but I had an idea of his great steadfastness and reliability. . . .

But our awareness of the earlier letters to Powell may make Dickens's attempt to distance himself from the offender seem somewhat disingenuous. ⟨. . .⟩

When Powell's forgery had first become known, in July 1846, Dickens seemed shocked and also eager to minimise whatever degree of friendship he had once maintained with this man. But from at least October 20, 1849, on, the novelist was infuriated at Powell, who had gratuitously attacked him, and this anger may have led to a change in the way in which Uriah Heep is depicted in numbers subsequently composed.

In *David Copperfield* Dickens does not introduce Heep until the novel is approximately one-fourth over. On first meeting Uriah, David immediately notices his unattractive appearance: 'a cadaverous face', 'hair . . . cropped as close as the closest stubble', 'hardly any eyebrows, and no eyelashes', 'a long, lank skeleton hand'. Even though Copperfield at this time has no other reason for disliking Heep, just the simple act of shaking hands proves distasteful: 'what a clammy hand this was!' Despite this reaction, however, David in the very next chapter, the first in the sixth installment, feels 'attracted towards Uriah Heep' and finds in him 'a sort of fascination', leading to a dream in which Uriah is a pirate threatening David and Em'ly. ⟨. . .⟩

When Dickens first began planning and writing *David Copperfield,* he probably saw Uriah not as in any way a reflection of Powell, but as a character akin to Fielding's Blifil in *Tom Jones,* a mean-spirited scoundrel who becomes the hero's sexual rival, or perhaps a figure like Joseph Surface in Sheridan's *A School for Scandal,* a hypocritical scandal-monger who expresses noble sentiments while being actually motivated by greed and lust. At this time, Thomas Powell, as we have observed, seemed merely to be an acquaintance whom Dickens was eager to forget. We may note, too, that Uriah is physically nearly the antithesis of Powell, who was in 'personal appearance . . . the conventional bluff, hearty, and bulky Englishman of the John Bull type.'

After Dickens's discovery, however, of the hitherto unsuspected hostility of Powell, we find various resemblances between the latter's career and Heep's. Either these are simply coincidences or else the novelist began seeing Powell as a model for some of the behaviour of Heep, another malicious, slandering, hypocritical forger and thief. As Forster observes, 'it is never anything complete that is thus taken from life by a genuine writer, but only leading traits, or such as may give greater finish; . . . the fine artist will embody in his portraiture of one person his experiences of fifty.'

Whatever the case, Dickens's synthesising art is so remarkable that Uriah remains a consistent character who is perfectly integrated into Copperfield's rich and complicated narrative. Because of overwhelming hostility towards the protagonist, Heep is prompted to steal from Aunt Betsey, an act that leads to her testing of David and the fateful shifting of his career from proctor to writer. Uriah may be seen, therfore, as ultimately helping David and further demonstrating that providence can make adversity beneficial, the theme of Agnes's important letter to Copperfield in Switzerland. If the venomous attack by Thomas Powell helped stimulate the development of Heep, we find another illustration of this principle in Dickens's own life.

—Stanley Friedman, "Heep and Powell: Dickensian Revenge?" *The Dickensian* 90, no. 1 (Spring 1994): pp. 36–42.

Plot Summary of
A Tale of Two Cities

The famous first sentence of Charles Dickens's *A Tale of Two Cities* establishes important thematic and structural patterns of the novel:

> It was the best of times, it was the worst of times, it was the age of wisdom, it was the age of foolishness, it was the epoch of belief, it was the epoch of incredulity, it was the season of Light, it was the season of Darkness, it was the spring of hope, it was the winter of despair, we had everything before us, we had nothing before us, we were all going direct to Heaven, we were all going direct the other way. . . .

Just as these phrases achieve their stirring rhetorical effect by broad conceptual oppositions, the novel as a whole achieves its vivid imaginative effects by means of starkly contrasting settings, personalities, and motivations: staid England and turbulent France; hopeful Charles Darnay and self-destructive Sydney Carton; tender Lucie Manette and bloodthirsty Madame Defarge. Even the resurrection and rejuvenation of Dr. Manette and Charles Darnay are contrasted with the destruction of countless innocent people by the cruelties first of France's Old Regime and then of the Republican terror. Dickens uses these contrasts to explore, in the context of revolutionary France, the subject that forms the center of his interest throughout his many novels: the effect large forces such as class, technology, and historical change have on human feeling and action.

Book one, **chapter one** evokes the uneasy mood that prevailed in England and France in 1775. Dickens describes it as a time of lawlessness and tyranny, brooding rebellion and apocalyptic prophecies. This mood is sustained throughout the novel as the narrative moves from the historical to the personal (**chapter two**). Mr. Jarvis Lorry, a passenger on the Dover mail coach, receives a dispatch from "T. and Co.:" "Wait at Dover for Mam'selle." His brief and enigmatic reply: "RECALLED TO LIFE." Lorry later dreams that he is digging someone out of a grave (**chapter three**): "I hope you care to live?" he asks the man he has rescued in his dream. "I can't say," the man replies.

In **chapter four** Mr. Lorry arrives at the Royal George Hotel in Dover, where he has arranged to meet Lucie Manette. He begins to tell a story, which the young woman, Lucie Manette, who remembers being brought to England by Mr. Lorry as a young child, quickly recognizes as that of her family.

Mr. Lorry tells Lucy about the Doctor of Beaufais, a Frenchman with an account at Tellson's (the bank, "T. & Co."), who suddenly vanished almost twenty years ago. The doctor seemed to have fallen prey to a powerful enemy who had the "privilege of filling up blank forms for the consignment of any one to the oblivion of a prison for any length of time." Even though the doctor's wife, an Englishwoman, searched for her husband until her death two years later, she raised their infant daughter to believe that her father was dead, hoping to spare her pain. He then tells the much shaken Lucie that Tellson's has found her father, who is under the care of a former servant in Paris. "We are going there," he tells her, "I, to identify him if I can: you, to restore him to life, love, duty, rest, comfort."

Chapter five shifts to the exterior of a Paris wineshop; red wine flows between the cobblestones from a broken cask. The poor people who live in the area use their hands to scoop the wine into their mouths. On a literal level, the image reflects the extreme degradation in which the common people of France live. On another level, the spilled wine foreshadows the human blood that will flow during the French Revolution. And on yet another level, the people's hands and garments are said to be "stained" by the wine—a term that suggests that the people are tainted or made guilty by their actions in the Revolution.

The wine also has a more positive religious connotation: The Christian ritual of resurrection and rebirth. In the Christian Mass, the transformation of ordinary wine into the blood of Jesus Christ commemorates his sacrifice for humankind. The wine thus has a double significance: It represents both Christ's suffering and his capacity to redeem humanity. Dickens weaves the Christian symbolism of resurrection throughout the novel, as in Mr. Lorry's odd message: "Recalled to Life."

Inside the wineshop, Mr. Lorry and Lucie observe a cryptic exchange between the proprietors, Monsieur and Madame Defarge, and several customers, who all address each other as Jacques. Mr. Lorry leads the pair to a room where they find a crazed white-haired man sitting on a low bench, making shoes. He tells them, in a "forlorn" voice, that his name is "One Hundred and Five, North Tower" (**chapter six**). Mr. Lorry addresses him by his former name, "Monsieur Manette," but fails to elicit any remembrance. Only at the sight of his daughter does the prisoner begin to show signs of recognition. He is still disoriented as they lead him to a waiting coach. Book one closes with Mr. Lorry's portentous question, "I hope you care to be recalled to life?" His answer is uncertain: "I can't say."

Book two, "The Golden Thread," takes up the story five years later. Mr. Lorry is attending the trial of Charles Darnay, a young French gentleman accused of betraying British secrets to the French king (**chapter two**). Lucie testifies that Darnay had traveled by ship with them when they returned from France five years before. On the stand Lucie recalls the tenderness with which the accused treated her ailing father but also admits that Darnay did confer with two Frenchmen before the ship departed. Darnay is acquitted.

In **chapter four** we learn that in the five years since his departure from France, Lucie's tender care has restored Dr. Manette to his former self and that Darnay has become a close friend of the family. In **chapter six** Mr. Lorry, having become friends with the Manettes, visits them in their home in Soho. Darnay arrives and tells a remarkable story about some workmen who found an old dungeon in the Tower of London where a prisoner, before going to execution, had carved the word DIG on the cornerstone. Upon examining the earth underneath the stone, they found the ashes of a paper, mingled with the ashes of a small leather case or bag. The paper, Darnay concludes, must have contained some vital information that the prisoner wished to hide from his jailers. After hearing the story, Dr. Manette becomes extremely agitated.

The novel shifts to France and focuses upon the decadent and despicable Marquis de St. Evrèmonde, a French nobleman (**chapters seven** through **nine**). Driving into the countryside from Paris, the marquis is forced to stop when his coach runs over and kills a child. As the father grieves, the marquis throws a gold coin toward the gathered peasants and castigates them for not taking better care of their children.

Eventually, the marquis arrives at an imposing stone chateau, where Charles Darnay meets him. Darnay heatedly argues with the marquis, who is his uncle (**chapter nine**). Because of his family's cruel behavior, Darnay has decided to renounce his name and inheritance; he will stay in England and work for his living. He warns his uncle that "there is a curse" on the ancestral lands and perhaps on all of France. The next morning the marquis is found with a knife in his heart. A note attached to the hilt of the knife suggests the act is revenge for the driving accident: "Drive him fast to his tomb. This, from JACQUES."

From this point to the end of the novel, the narrative splits into two strands; one takes place in England, the other in France. Much of the action in England revolves around the courtship and marriage of Lucie. Darnay, now a teacher, is in love with Lucie and approaches her father about marriage (**chapter ten**). But Dr. Manette is hesitant, so Darnay requests only that if Lucie asks about him, she should be told of his desire to marry her. Dr. Manette agrees on the condition that, if they do marry, Darnay will not tell him his real last name until the morning of their wedding.

Lucie and Darnay marry (**chapter seventeen**) but, as soon as they have departed, Dr. Manette lapses into his fit of shoemaking, which lasts for ten days. The doctor assures Mr. Lorry that his problem is unlikely to arise again (**chapter nineteen**). The couple returns and settles into a peaceful life. They have a son and a daughter; only the daughter survives (**chapters twenty** and **twenty-one**).

The second strand of the narrative describes the rising rage and resentment in France (**chapter fifteen**). We return to the Paris wineshop, where Mme. Defarge sits, like a Greek fate, tirelessly knitting. By this, Dickens suggests that no action or event is historically inconsequential, but is instead part of a larger pattern.

After a year, the enraged father who vengefully killed the marquis was apprehended and hanged. As are many of his compatriots, M. Defarge is impatient for revenge against the Evrèmonde family. Mme. Defarge urges him to be patient. As the voice of historical fate, she knows that vengeance is inevitable, but must occur only at the proper time.

In **chapter twenty-one** the two narrative strands begin to come together. The first half of the chapter focuses upon the Darnays, while the second half describes the storming of the Bastille, which begins the French Revolution. M. Defarge is at the head of the mob storming the prison and goes directly to Dr. Manette's old cell, which he tears apart in a frantic search for an unidentified object. Then, with M. Defarge leading the way, the mob embarks on a spree of violence. An aristocrat is hanged and beheaded (**chapter twenty-two**) and the chateau of the Marquis de St. Evrèmonde is burned (**chapter twenty-three**).

The Revolution roars wildly in France for three years while the Darnays continue to live peacefully in London (**chapter twenty-four**). Mr. Lorry leaves for Paris to recover some of Tellson's important papers; Darnay follows him, sending word to Lucie and Dr. Manette that he will write them when he arrives (**chapter twenty-five**).

Darnay is captured on his way to Paris by a mob that curses him as an aristocrat (**book three, chapter one**). Over the next year and several months Dr. Manette keeps Charles, still imprisoned, from being beheaded and aids the wounded and sick from both sides. By **chapter thirteen** Darnay, found guilty at trial, awaits execution. An old rival, for Lucie and in business, comes to Darnay's cell, knocks him unconscious, and has him dragged out of the cell to Mr. Lorry's waiting carriage. The man, Carton, disguises himself as Darnay and goes to the guillotine in his place (**chapter fifteen**).

Carton's famous final works capture the spiritual and emotional redemption he achieves through his self-sacrifice: "It is a far, far better thing that I do, than I have ever done; it is a far, far better rest that I go to than I have ever known." His action and his words recall the imagery of resurrection and renewal that recur throughout the novel. In accordance with the Christian economy of sacrifice, Carton must lose his life in order to find it. Similarly, France must tear itself down in order to rise again. ✸

List of Characters in
A Tale of Two Cities

Charles Darnay is a descendant of the French noble family of St. Evrèmonde. Horrified by his family's history of cruelty and repression, he moves to England, changes his name, establishes himself as a teacher of French language and literature, and marries Lucie Manette. He is drawn back to revolutionary France by the appeal of a former servant. There he is captured and sentenced to death as an aristocrat and emigrant by the revolutionary mob. Only the self-sacrifice of a rival suitor of Lucie saves him from the guillotine.

Sydney Carton is a bright but moody and dissipated legal assistant to a successful London lawyer, Mr. Stryver. Unable to win the heart of the woman he loves (Lucie Manette), he leads a life of slovenly despair. He redeems himself finally by giving up his own life so that Lucie's husband, Charles Darnay, might live.

Lucie Manette is the sweet-tempered daughter of Dr. Manette, who was imprisoned in the Bastille for twenty years. When he is rescued, she nurses him back to psychological health. She marries Charles Darnay, with whom she has two children, one of whom dies. It is through love for her that Sydney Carton sacrifices his life to save Charles Darnay.

Dr. Manette is a decent and competent French doctor who is imprisoned in the Bastille for twenty years by the Old Regime. While in prison he learns the craft of shoemaking and writes a detailed account of the cruelties he saw performed by the members of the aristocratic St. Evrèmonde family. This account is later used to denounce his own innocent son-in-law, Charles Darnay.

Jarvis Lorry is a fastidious, diplomatic, and well-respected businessman and bachelor. He works for Tellson's, the London bank that handles the accounts of many members of the French aristocracy. He takes Dr. Manette's daughter out of France after her father is imprisoned, later returning to rescue him as well. He remains a close friend of the Manette family and is instrumental in the final rescue of Charles Darnay.

Madame Defarge is the novel's symbol of fate. With her husband she leads the revolutionary movement in Paris from their wineshop. Implacable and relentless, she is consumed by the desire for revenge against the aristocratic regime that tortured and killed members of her family. She compulsively knits a chronicle of the significant events of the Revolution.

Monsieur Defarge is the husband of Madame Defarge, co-owner of the wineshop, and co-leader of the revolutionary movement in Paris. He is equally unforgiving and even more impatient for revenge than his wife.

The Marquis de St. Evrèmonde (Monseigneur), the uncle of Charles Darnay, embodies the vices of the French aristocracy in the eighteenth century. Cruel, selfish, and arrogant, he treats the common people of France like animals. He is assassinated by the father of a peasant child whom he carelessly rode over in his carriage.

Miss Pross is the sturdy and loyal maid of Lucie Manette. She believes that no one is good enough to marry Lucie except her long-lost brother, Solomon, who turns out to be a spy. She kills the fearful Mme. Defarge at the end of the novel.

Solomon Pross/John Barsad is the ne'er-do-well brother of Miss Pross. Her high regard for him notwithstanding, he takes her money, disappears, and reappears years later, first as a spy for the English government, then as a spy for the revolutionary government in France. Carton sees through his double cross and blackmails him into helping rescue Charles Darnay.

Jerry Cruncher is the rough-hewn messenger and handyman for Tellson's. He moonlights as a "resurrection man"—digging up dead bodies for pay. ❀

Critical Views on
A Tale of Two Cities

JOHN GROSS ON CARTON AND DARNAY

[John Gross, an editorial consultant for the *Observer* (London) and a member of the editorial staff of the *New York Times Book Review*, has written critical studies of John P. Marquand (1963) and James Joyce (1970) as well as *The Rise and Fall of the Man of Letters* (1969). In this extract, Gross maintains that *A Tale of Two Cities* is structured around the figures of Carton and Darnay, who respectively represent the wastrel and the hero in the novel.]

A Tale of Two Cities is a tale of two heroes. The theme of the double has such obvious attractions for a writer preoccupied with disguises, rival impulses, and hidden affinities that it is surprising that Dickens didn't make more use of it elsewhere. But no one could claim that his handling of the device is very successful here, or that he has managed to range the significant forces of the novel behind Carton and Darnay. Darnay is, so to speak, the accredited representative of Dickens in the novel, the 'normal' hero for whom a happy ending is still possible. It has been noted, interestingly enough, that he shares his creator's initials—and that is pretty well the only interesting thing about him. Otherwise he is a pasteboard character, completely undeveloped. His position as an exile, his struggles as a language-teacher, his admiration for George Washington are so many openings thrown away.

Carton, of course, is a far more striking figure. He belongs to the line of cultivated wastrels who play an increasingly large part in Dickens's novels during the second half of his career, culminating in Eugene Wrayburn; his clearest predecessor, as his name indicates, is the luckless Richard Carstone of *Bleak House*. He has squandered his gifts and drunk away his early promise; his will is broken, but his intellect is unimpaired. In a sense, his opposite is not Darnay at all, but the aggressive Stryver, who makes a fortune by picking his brains. Yet there is something hollow about his complete resignation to failure: his self-abasement in front of Lucie, for instance. ("I am like one who died young ... I know very well that you can have no tenderness for me ...") For, stagy a figure though he is, Carton does suggest what Thomas

Hardy calls 'fearful unfulfilments'; he still has vitality, and it is hard to believe that he has gone down without a struggle. The total effect is one of energy held unnaturally in check: the bottled-up frustration which Carton represents must spill over somewhere.

Carton's and Darnay's fates are entwined from their first meeting, at the Old Bailey trial. Over the dock there hangs a mirror: 'crowds of the wicked and the wretched had been reflected in it, and had passed from its surface and this earth's together. Haunted in a most ghastly manner that abominable place would have been, if the glass could ever have rendered back its reflections, as the ocean is one day to give up its dead.' After Darnay's acquittal we leave him with Carton, 'so like each other in feature, so unlike in manner, both reflected in the glass above them'. Reflections, like ghosts, suggest unreality and self-division, and at the end of the same day Carton stares at his own image in the glass and upbraids it: 'Why should you particularly like a man who resembles you? There is nothing in you to like: you know that. Ah, confound you! . . . Come on, and have it out in plain words! You hate the fellow.' In front of the mirror, Carton thinks of changing places with Darnay; at the end of the book, he is to take the other's death upon him. Dickens prepares the ground: when Darnay is in jail, it is Carton who strikes Mr. Lorry as having 'the wasted air of a prisoner', and when he is visited by Carton on the rescue attempt, he thinks at first that he is 'an apparition of his own imagining'. But Dickens is determined to stick by Darnay: a happy ending *must* be possible. As Lorry and his party gallop to safety with the drugged Darnay, there is an abrupt switch to the first person: 'The wind is rushing after us, and the clouds are flying after us, and the moon is plunging after us, and the whole wild night is in pursuit of us; but so far, we are pursued by nothing else.' We can make our escape, however narrowly; Carton, expelled from our system, must be abandoned to his fate.

But the last word is with Carton—the most famous last word in Dickens, in fact. Those who take a simplified view of Dickens's radicalism, or regard him as one of nature's Marxists, can hardly help regretting that *A Tale of Two Cities* should end as it does. They are bound to feel, with Edgar Johnson, that 'instead of merging, the truth of revolution and the truth of sacrifice are made to appear in conflict'. A highly personal, indeed a unique crisis cuts across public issues and muffles the political message. But this is both to sentimentalize Dickens's view of the revolution, and to miss the point about Carton.

The cynical judgment that his sacrifice was trifling, since he had nothing to live for, is somewhat nearer the mark. Drained of the will to live, he is shown in the closing chapters of the book as a man courting death, and embracing it when it comes. 'In seasons of pestilence, some of us will have a secret attraction to the disease—a terrible passing inclination to die of it. And all of us have like wonders hidden in our breasts, only needing circumstances to evoke them.' It is Carton rather than Darnay who is 'drawn to the loadstone rock.' On his last walk around Paris, a passage which Shaw cites in the preface to *Man and Superman* as proof of Dickens's essentially irreligious nature, his thoughts run on religion: 'I am the Resurrection and the Life.' But his impressions are all of death: the day comes coldly, 'looking like a dead face out of the sky', while on the river 'a trading boat, with a sail of the softened colour of a dead leaf, then glided into his view, floated by him, and died away'. His walk recalls an earlier night, when he wandered round London with wreaths of dust spinning round and round before the morning blast, as if the desert sand had risen far away and the first spray of it in its advance had begun to overwhelm the city'. Then, with the wilderness bringing home to him a sense of the wasted powers within him, he saw a momentary mirage of what he might have achieved and was reduced to tears; but now that the city has been over-whelmed in earnest, he is past thinking of what might have been. 'It is a far, far better thing that I do, than I have ever done'—but the 'better thing' might just as well be committing suicide as laying down his life for Darnay. At any rate, he thinks of himself as going towards rest, not towards resurrection.

—John Gross, "*A Tale of Two Cities*," *Dickens and the Twentieth Century*, ed. John Gross and Gabriel Pearson (London: Routledge & Kegan Paul, 1962): pp. 189–192.

☙

EARLE DAVIS ON CARLYLE'S INFLUENCE ON DICKENS

[Earle Davis, a former professor of English at Kansas State University, is the author of *Vision Fugitive: Ezra Pound and Economics* (1968) and *The Flint and the Flame: The Artistry of*

Defarge and his wife come indirectly from Carlyle. The history presents Santerre, a brewer, living in Saint-Antoine, who became a leader of the revolt, and Carlyle makes casual mention of the president of the Jacobin Society, whose name was Lafarge. A certain Usher Maillard was active in the storming of the Bastille, doing most of what Defarge did in Dickens' narrative. "Defarge" combines from these originals whatever the novelist needed for his action. Carlyle also devoted eleven chapters in his history of the early rioting to "The Insurrection of the Women." One of his female leaders, a black Joan of Arc, was Demoiselle Théroigne, a striking and spectacular mob captain. In the fight at the Tuileries, Carlyle describes her as *Sibyl* Théroigne: "Vengeance, *Victoire ou la mort!*" Mme. Defarge is not "small-waisted," but she performs as mob leader, being much more ruthless than her husband. Dickens also invents a character, a companion of Mme. Defarge, whom he designates only as The Vengeance. He took what he wanted from Carlyle, changed and concentrated it, and dressed up the details of his story from the historical record.

Carlyle attributes the worst excesses of the mob to the Jacobins, or the *Jacquerie*. Dickens creates types of revolt leaders from the lowest classes, giving them the names of Jacques One, Jacques Two, Jacques Three. The insignia of the French Revolution was patterned in threes—witness the tricolor and the slogan, "Liberty, Fraternity, and Equality." The Jacobin women were especially prominent at the guillotine, too, and the stories of their knitting while watching the executions were famous. Carlyle describes them at the executions, and Dickens applies this graphic bit of data to Mme. Defarge's knitted record of victims, handwork in which the names of the doomed were entwined with vengeance in her own variety of shorthand. The women are there knitting when Carton dies.

Names occasionally wander from one book to the other, perhaps in some entirely different connection from the original, showing merely that the name remained in Dickens' mind and was appropriated because the novelist needed some kind of cognomen. The hated *gabelle*, France's salt tax, turns up as the name of Darnay's agent on Monseigneur's estate, the man whose letter to Darnay begging his assistance in his trial is the excuse for tempting Darnay back to France and his capture. Carlyle casually mentions Thelusson's Bank, where the great Necker was once a clerk. Dickens, needing a name for the agency which served to bring Lucy Manette and later her father from France to England, shifted the establishment to Tellson's Bank, with branches in Paris as well as London.

Carlyle's description of the butchery which went on outside La Force Prison in the September Massacres of 1792 is about as horrible as anything in his chamber of hyperbolic horrors. Wanton and brutal slaying in the streets with axe and sword is much more forthright than death under the guillotine. Dickens describes the great grindstone in the yard outside the quarters of Tellson's Bank in Paris where the mob, shirts and clothing dripping with the blood of their victims, comes to sharpen weapons blunted in the awful slaughter.

Much of this transposition is the routine custom of the historical novelist, taking his details from a reputable source and supplying his facts where they are needed in his story. Of more interest to the critic of narrative technique are the instances in which only a suggestion is in the source, Dickens' expansion adding to the picture or the characterization which becomes an important part of his story. Dr. Manette, for example, lost his mind in the long years of confinement. He learned the shoemaker's trade in prison, and although nursed back to health and sanity upon coming to England, he suffers lapses of memory and reverts to his prison occupation whenever he is seriously troubled. This regression happens when Lucy marries Darnay and again when all seems lost and Darnay is sentenced to die.

—Earle Davis, *The Flint and the Flame: The Artistry of Charles Dickens* (Columbia: University of Missouri Press, 1963): pp. 247–248.

℘

ROBERT ALTER ON VIOLENCE IN *A TALE OF TWO CITIES*

[Robert Alter is a widely published critic and the author of *Fielding and the Nature of the Novel* (1968), *The Pleasures of Reading in an Ideological Age* (1989), and several books on the Bible and on American Jewish literature. He is a professor of Hebrew and comparative literature at the University of California at Berkeley. In this extract, Alter asserts that, although Dickens attempted to portray the potential of human regeneration in *A Tale of Two Cities*, it is the many scenes of revolutionary violence that remain most clearly in our minds.]

What Dickens is ultimately concerned with in *A Tale of Two Cities* is not a particular historical event—that is simply his chosen dramatic setting—but rather the relationship between history and evil, how violent oppression breeds violent rebellion which becomes a new kind of oppression. His account of the *ancien régime* and the French Revolution is a study in civilized man's vocation for proliferating moral chaos, and in this one important regard the *Tale* is the most compelling "modern" of his novels. He also tries hard, through the selfless devotion of his more exemplary characters, to suggest something of mankind's potential for moral regeneration; but he is considerably less convincing in this effort, partly because history itself offers so little evidence which the imagination of hope can use to sustain itself.

The most powerful imaginings of the novel reach out again and again to touch ultimate possibilities of violence, whether in the tidal waves of mass destruction or in the hideous inventiveness of individual acts of cruelty. In the first chapter we are introduced to France through the detailed description of an execution by horrible mutilation, and to England by a rapid series of images of murder, mob violence, and hangings. Throughout the novel, the English mob is in potential what the French revolutionary hordes are in bloody fact. At the English trial of the falsely accused Darnay, the "ogreish" spectators, eagerly awaiting the condemnation, vie with one another in their lip-smacking description of how a man looks being drawn and quartered. Again in France, the details of torture and savagery exercise an obscure fascination over the imagination of the characters (and perhaps of the writer as well)—nightmarish images of tongues torn out with pincers, gradual dismemberment, boiling oil and lead poured into gaping wounds, float through the darkness of the novel and linger on the retina of the memory.

The energy of destruction that gathers to such acts of concentrated horror pulses through the whole world of the novel, pounding at its foundations. It is conceived as an elemental force in nature which works through men as well. Dover Beach as Jarvis Lorry contemplates it near the beginning of the novel is a replica in nature of the revolution to come, the scene most strikingly serving as event: "the sea did what it liked, and what it liked was destruction. It thundered at the town, and thundered at the cliffs, and brought the coast down madly." The image of the revolutionary mob, much later in the novel, is simply the obverse of this vision of the ocean as chaos and darkness: "The sea of black and threatening waters, and of destructive upheaving of wave against wave, whose depths were yet unfathomed and whose forces were yet unknown. The remorseless sea of turbulently swaying shapes, voices of vengeance." These same pitiless forces are present in the rainstorm that descends upon the quiet Soho home of the Manettes as Lucie, Darnay, and Carton watch: the lightning, harbinger of revolution, that they see leaping from the stormy dark is the only light that can be born from the murky atmosphere of this world—the hot light of destruction. Later the revolution is also likened to a great earthquake, and when Madame Defarge adds to this her grim declaration—"Tell wind and fire where to stop . . . but don't tell me"—all four elements of the traditional world-picture have been associated with the forces of blind destruction, earth and water and fire and air.

There is, ultimately, a peculiar impersonality about this novel, for it is intended to dramatize the ways in which human beings become the slaves of impersonal forces, at last are made inhuman by them. In order to show the play of these elemental forces in history, Dickens adopts a generalizing novelistic technique which frequently approaches allegory, the mode of imagination traditionally used for the representation of cosmic powers doing battle or carrying out a destined plan. The Darkness and Light of the novel's first sentence are almost immediately supported by the introduction of two explicitly allegorical figures in the same chapter: the Woodman, Fate; and the Farmer, Death. In the action that follows, events and characters often assume the symbolic postures and formal masks of allegory.

—Robert Alter, "The Demons of History in Dickens's *Tale*" (1969), *Motives for Fiction* (Cambridge, MA: Harvard University Press, 1984), pp. 106–108.

EDWIN M. EIGNER ON DARNAY AS A REVOLUTIONARY
HERO

[Edwin M. Eigner is a former professor of English at the University of California at Riverside and the author of *The Metaphysical Novel in England and America* (1978) and *The Dickens Pantomime* (1989). In this extract, taken from an issue of *Dickens Studies Annual* largely devoted to *A Tale of Two Cities*, Eigner studies the figure of Darnay, finding him not fully filling the role of a Revolutionary hero because Dickens himself did not believe in such a figure.]

⟨H⟩ow much of Charles Darnay's guilt is not only an expression of the condition of man after the Fall and of undeniable psychological trauma, but is caused and perhaps justified by Charles's failures as social man?

To begin with, he has not fulfilled the first charge of his life, to sell his mother's jewels and give the money to the sister of the raped peasant girl, Madame Defarge, as it turns out. In fact, we are not told that Charles so much as made an attempt at carrying out this obligation, although it is possible that this is what he was trying to do on those mysterious trips between England and France between 1775 and 1780. This is special pleading in Charles's behalf, for there is no evidence, but I can think of no other explanation for the secrecy of these journeys, a secrecy which, at his English trial for treason, Charles maintains at very serious expense to his case and danger to his life. He told Lucie he "was travelling under an assumed name" because he "was travelling on a business of a delicate and difficult nature, which might get people into trouble." He could not have been divesting himself of his estate, for he had not come into that yet, and it is difficult to imagine who, besides himself and anti-aristocratic agents helping in the search for the wronged girl, might be in any danger. Still it is curious that Dickens maintains the secrecy, and curious also that Darnay, usually so apt to feel guilty, does not torture himself about this failure to carry out his mother's first command.

On the other hand, Darnay is distraught at his powerlessness to, as he says, "execute the last request of my dear mother's lips, and obey the last look of my dear mother's eyes, which implored me to have mercy and to redress." The powerlessness comes, presumably, from Charles's situation of having been passed over in the inheritance—his wicked uncle rules instead of him—but when he does succeed to the estate, just hours after making this speech, he is still unable to perform effectively:

> he had acted imperfectly. He knew very well, that in his love for Lucie, his renunciation of his social place, though by no means new to his mind, had been hurried and incomplete. He knew that he ought to have systematically worked it out and supervised it, and that he had meant to do it, and that it had never been done. . . . he had watched the times for a time of action . . . until the time had gone by.

But even this confession of failure by Charles misses the point. Presumably his mother's lips and eyes had not implored him to renounce his power, but rather to use it for the sake of the poor.

Nevertheless, the sense of guilt and shame called up by this train of thought impels Charles's return to France for the sake of saving his servant and using his influence to moderate the revolution. Dickens writes "His latent uneasiness had been, that bad aims were being worked out in his own unhappy land by bad instruments, and that he, who could not fail to know that he was better than they, was not there, trying to do something to stay the bloodshed, and assert the claims of mercy and humanity." All very fine, but painful though it is to contradict T. A. Jackson, perhaps the one critic who has something positive to say about Charles, I am not sure Dickens wants us entirely to admire the "large-hearted generosity" of his hero when he sends him back to France, drawn to the loadstone rock. In the first place, he is still not acting to redress as his mother had commanded but only to plead mercy for the members and the agents of his own class. As his assumed name suggests, and it has to be significant in a novel filled with Carlyle's clothing symbols and with symbolic names, Charles Darnay is, at best, a mender, and has no place as part of a revolution. He wants reform; the Defarges, true revolutionaries, want continued abuses to infuriate the people.

In the second place, Charles's impulsive action is strongly reminiscent of the ineffective or unsustained windmill charges on social institutions made by previous romantic heroes in Dickens's novels. He dashes into the French Revolution as Arthur Clennam of *Little Dorrit* took on the Circumlocution Office or as Richard Carstone of *Bleak House* smashed his head against the Court of Chancery. The action is naively vain, as Dickens suggests when he tells us of Darnay that the "glorious vision of doing good, which is so often the sanguine mirage of so many good minds, arose before him, and he even saw himself in the illusion with some influence to guide this raging Revolution." And there is also the possibility of an unworthy subconscious motivation for his action. Since it developed from a sense of shame and guilt, Charles's purpose, like that of Clennam, may be to punish himself. Having failed to redress the wrong as his mother had charged him to do, he may be embracing the opportunity for the violent atonement she had predicted as the alternative. In any event, these are the ways Charles's brief career as a social activist seems destined to turn out— vain and self-destructive.

But before we go too far in joining the chorus which condemns Charles Darnay, it is well to remember that Dickens could never bring himself to believe in the Carlylean hero and that by this time in his career he was highly skeptical of the effectuality of social action of any sort. Dickens may not be criticizing Charles Darnay's qualities as a Revolutionary hero; he is more likely undermining the very concept of romantic heroism by doubting both its motives and its possibilities for success. Charles is at least as powerless in Revolutionary France as he was in bourgeois England, but in the long run he is no less effectual than the other would-be Revolutionary heroes whose fate Carton predicts in the final chapter.

—Edwin M. Eigner, "Charles Darnay and Revolutionary Identity," *Dickens Studies Annual* 12 (1983): pp. 154–156.

J. M. Rignall on the Contradictory Nature of the Novel

[J. M. Rignall is a professor of English at the University of Warwick in Coventry, England. He has written *Realist Fiction and the Strolling Spectator* (1992). In this extract, Rignall believes that there is a contradiction at the heart of *A Tale of Two Cities* between the inevitability of violence in history and a hope that violence can be ended or averted by self-sacrifice.]

It is not surprising that the most remembered scene in *A Tale of Two Cities* is the last, for this novel is dominated, even haunted, by its ending. From the opening chapter in which the "creatures of this chronicle" are set in motion "along the roads that lay before them," while the Woodman Fate and the Farmer Death go silently about their ominous work, those roads lead with sinister inevitability to the revolutionary scaffold. To an unusual extent, especially given the expansive and centrifugal nature of Dickens's imagination, this is an end-determined narrative whose individual elements are ordered by an ending which is both their goal and, in a sense, their source. In a historical novel like this there is a transparent relationship between narrative form and historical vision, and the formal features of *A Tale*—its emphatic linearity, continuity, and negative teleology—define a distinctive vision of history. As Robert Alter has argued in his fine critical account of the novel, it is not the particular historical event that ultimately concerns Dickens here, but rather a wider view of history and the historical process. That process is a peculiarly grim one. As oppression is shown to breed oppression, violence to beget violence, evil to provoke evil, a pattern emerges that is too deterministic to owe much to Carlyle and profoundly at odds with the conventional complacencies of Whig history. Instead of progress there is something more like the catastrophic continuum that is Walter Benjamin's description of the historical process: the single catastrophe, piling wreckage upon wreckage. And when, in the sentimental postscript of Carton's prophecy, Dickens finally attempts to envisage a liberation from this catastrophic process, he can only do so, like Benjamin, in eschatological terms. For Benjamin it was the messianic intervention of a proletarian revolution that would bring time to a standstill and blast open the continuum of history; for Dickens it is the Christ-like intervention of a self-sacrificing individual that is the vehicle for a vision of a better world which seems to lie beyond time and history. The parallel with Benjamin cannot be pressed beyond the common perception of a pernicious historical continuum and the common desire to break it, but the coexistence of these two elements in *A Tale* is, I wish to argue, important for an understanding of the novel, lending it a peculiarly haunted and contradictory quality as Dickens gives expression to a vision of history which both compels and repels him at the same time.

In Carton's final vision of a world seemingly beyond time, the paradigm of the apocalypse mediates between what is known of history and what may be hoped for it. That hope is not to be dismissed as mere sentimentality, whatever the manner of its expression. However inadequately realized Carton's prophecy may be in imaginative terms, it is significant as a moment of resistance to the grimly terminal linearity and historical determinism of the preceding narrative. That resistance is not confined to the last page of the novel, for, as I shall show, it manifests itself in other places and in other ways, creating a faint but discernible counter-current to the main thrust of the narrative. This is not to say that Dickens presents a thorough-going deconstruction of his own narrative procedures and version of history in A Tale, for the process at work here is more ambiguous and tentative than that. There is a struggle with sombre fears that gives rise to contradictions which cannot be reduced to the internal self-contradictions of language. What the novel presents is, rather, the spectacle of an imagination both seized by a compelling vision of history as a chain of violence, a catastrophic continuum, and impelled to resist that vision in the very act of articulation, so that the narrative seems at the same time to seek and to shun the violent finality of its ending in the Terror. The nightmare vision is too grim to accept without protest, and too powerful to be dispelled by simple hopefulness, and the work bears the signs of this unresolved and unresolvable contradiction.

—J. M. Rignall, "Dickens and the Catastrophic Continuum of History in A Tale of Two Cities," ELH 51, no. 3 (Fall 1984): pp. 575–576.

RUTH GLANCY ON LUCY MANETTE

[Ruth Glancy, a lecturer in English at Concordia College in Edmonton, Alberta, Canada, is the author of bibliographies of Dickens's Christmas books (1985) and of A Tale of Two Cities (1993) as well as a study of that novel, from which the following extract is taken. Here, Glancy focuses on the figure of Lucie Manette, finding her centrally related to all the characters in the book.]

When Dickens suggested "The Thread of Gold" for the title of the novel, he was intending it to be Lucie Manette's story. And in many ways it is. The Bastille prisoner is recalled to life through her agency;

Darnay's new life is bound up with hers; Carton is inspired to his supreme sacrifice because of his love for her and his recognition of her goodness. She is central to the actions of nearly all the characters except perhaps the Crunchers: Mr. Lorry is devoted to her and acts throughout the novel largely out of this devotion; Miss Pross too is governed in her actions solely by her love of Lucie. Madame Defarge directs her anger against Lucie because she is Darnay's wife and because she therefore represents the aristocratic wife whose death will somehow compensate for the sufferings of the peasant wives and children. In many ways the characters are also paired around the central figure of Lucie. Miss Pross is pitted against Madame Defarge, and their final fatal meeting is caused by Miss Pross's attempts to prevent Madame Defarge from finding Lucie and condemning her to the tribunal. Carton and Darnay, physical doubles, are rivals for Lucie's love. Stryver and Carton both aspire to her hand, but Carton's unselfish love for her is contrasted with Stryver's selfish desire to own a wife as he would a piece of property. Darnay and Manette love her enough to share her because, as Darnay tells her, she is able to spare enough of herself to keep everyone happy.

We have seen how Lucie's characterization derived from Dickens's childhood friend Lucy Stroughill, his golden-haired neighbor, and the golden-haired Lucy from *The Wreck of the Golden Mary* who, like Lucie Manette, is the inspiration that keeps hope alive in the desperate survivors of the shipwreck. "Lucie" means light, and both characters take on a religious significance as the possessors of a spiritual purity. The golden thread too has religious connotations. It is traditionally a metaphor for the inviolable heart of things, the sacred core of truth and honesty that binds together the more vulnerable pieces of the fabric. In English law it refers to the tenet that a man is innocent until he is proven guilty. Without the golden thread, any other virtues in the system cannot survive. And so it is with Lucie, who gives meaning and purpose to the lives of Darnay, Carton, Manette, Miss Pross, and Mr. Lorry. There are many connecting threads in the book, such as Manette's connection to Darnay and the Defarges, but whereas these threads lead to the revelation of hidden sufferings and repressed guilt, Lucie's golden thread binds the characters into an indestructible web of love that will prove stronger than Madame Defarge's powerful lust for revenge. ⟨ . . . ⟩

Lucie has been criticized as being a faceless character, too good to be true and lacking in dimension. Certainly her speech is often ludicrously stagy, as in her first long address to her father when the refrain "weep for it" merely adds to the sentimentality of her words. Her conversation with Carton is equally melodramatic. But we have already seen how Dickens intended the characters to be "true to nature, but whom the story should express more than they should express themselves by dialogue" (John Forster). Seen through her actions, Lucie is anything but a melodramatic stage heroine; rather, she is a courageous woman like the British women caught in the bloodbath of the Indian Massacre whom Dickens wanted to honor in *The Perils of Certain English Prisoners.* Heroic women took an increasingly major role in Dickens's later novels, perhaps through the influence of Ellen Ternan. Ellen had played the part of another heroic Lucy, Lucy Crawford in *The Frozen Deep,* and Dickens certainly was thinking of her when he named Estella in *Great Expectations* and Helena Landless in *Edwin Drood* (Ellen's middle name was Lawless). Lucie's bravery is the determined but patient courage that Dickens talked of as "quiet heroism" in *The Battle of Life.* Like Little Dorrit in the novel preceding *A Tale of Two Cities,* Lucie is the sole support of an imprisoned and sometimes mentally deranged father. Although she fears the footsteps that seem to be threatening Soho and dreads the shadow that Madame Defarge casts over her, she is resilient enough to brave the dangerous streets of Paris to stand beneath the prison wall every day, in the hopes that Darnay may see her there. The thread of gold that binds her to him would lead her, as Carton tells Mr. Lorry, to "lay her own fair head beside her husband's cheerfully" on the guillotine. Lucie's role in the book is to provide the moral center from which the people surrounding her draw their strength. She is less active than the later heroines of *Our Mutual Friend* and *Edwin Drood,* Lizzie Hexam and Helena Landless, because that sort of tough, aggressive woman is seen in Miss Pross and taken to horrifying extremes in Madame Defarge. Lizzie Hexam rescues Eugene Wrayburn (a dissolute waster like Carton) from drowning because she is a skillful oarswoman and is able to pull him to safety. Because Madame Defarge and Miss Pross share this physical strength, Lucie's strength is mental and emotional, but she exemplifies the qualities of a genuine hero: strength, dedication, patience, and bravery.

—Ruth Glancy, A Tale of Two Cities: *Dickens's Revolutionary Novel* (Boston: Twayne, 1991): pp. 94–97.

[Tom Lloyd is a professor of English at Georgia Southern University and the author of articles on Dickens and Carlyle. In this extract, Lloyd, studying the character of Madame Defarge, believes that she is a kind of force of nature parallel to the Revolution itself.]

Madame Defarge embodies in its most absolute form the inevitable release of what Schiller terms the 'crude, lawless instincts' of those repressed politically and psychologically. Based on Mlle Théroigne in Carlyle's *The French Revolution,* she is like a force of nature whose instinctual patience is indicated by the 'register' she stores in her memory of who is to be saved and who executed once the energies of Saint Antoine are unleashed to sweep away the enervated aristocracy. Madame Defarge seems conscious of the natural energy she represents, consistently comparing the Revolution to a natural force and denying that it can be quantified or defined. For example, she tells her more conventional husband that 'it does not take a long time . . . for an earthquake to swallow a town,' but stresses the inadequacy of formulas in adding the question, 'Tell me how long it takes to prepare the earthquake?' She refuses to try to hurry the time of vengeance, saying that 'When the time comes, let loose a tiger and a devil; but wait for the time with the tiger and the devil chained.'

M Defarge retains a need for clear definitions and manifestations of things, which his wife recognizes, telling him, 'you sometimes need to see your victim and your opportunity, to sustain you.' She regards as a weakness his desire to know when the violence will begin and end, insisting that such quantification is impossible, like trying 'to make and store the lightning.' Psychologically in a realm beyond formulas, she cannot set limits to her philosophy of 'extermination', and therefore opposes her husband's assertion that the Terror 'must stop somewhere.' But M Defarge seeks meanings even when he participates in the storming of the Bastille. Though no one is presently in the North Tower where Manette was imprisoned for eighteen years, he demands that one of the guards take him there so that he can understand the meaning of One Hundred and Five: 'Does it mean a captive, or a place of captivity? Or do you mean that I shall strike you dead?' In an environment where identities are scrambled or extinguished and people are reduced to 'ghosts' of their former selves, Defarge wants a clear definition of the mystery called Manette. The 'indifference' of the Marquis and the 'absolute' extermination of Madame Defarge are antitypes of the endeavour to connect words with things. Defarge's violent destruction of the furniture in Manette's old cell to find a written or other key to his mystery reflects a paradoxical desire to obliterate and know; we later discover that he found the manuscript in the chimney, a place of ashes as well as energy. His search is normally fruitless, for he finds only a dead text which no longer reflects the spiritual essence of its author.

In *A Tale of Two Cities* there is a non-verbal communication based on vengeance, and another based on love. Madame Defarge repudiates formulas in favour of absolute violence and mysterious signs based on knitting, roses in handkerchiefs, and noncommittal allusions to natural forces. But at a time when the word is falsified and dead, such signs are more efficacious than M Defarge's futile search for definitions amidst the carnage at the Bastille. Those able to read history—Dickens places his reader in this advantaged position—can read the non-verbal message contained in the Cross of Blood drawn in the air by Madame Defarge's brother, or the verbal sign BLOOD Gaspard scrawls on a wall with wine. But there are also transcendent non-verbal signs based on love and sympathy, for instance in the eyes of Darnay's mother, which give meaning to her assertion that he must 'have mercy and redress' the wrongs perpetrated by his family on the poor. Above all, Lucie Manette has this ability. By standing outside Darnay's Paris prison she can revitalize him, reversing his initial, precipitous slide into insanity. Madame Defarge's inability to comprehend this alternative form of communication is revealed by her plot to denounce Lucie for 'making signs and signals to prisoners.'

Yet she is forced to effect a non-verbal communication with Miss Pross in the climactic scene where the sans-culotte comes hunting for Lucie, who is in the process of escaping from Paris. Here her energies are thwarted, and she is spent like any natural storm or earthquake. The cessation of her power through Pross's pistol shot foreshadows the retreat of the violently daemonic and the reconstitution of the word, symbolized by the power of the signed papers to get Darnay (disguised as Carton), Manette, and Lucie out of the country. Like Thomas Mann's demonic Cipolla, Defarge is suddenly rendered lifeless, as though a violent disrobing of civilized control and language have played themselves out, leaving Pross deaf but free. In this grotesque encounter the two cannot understand each other's words: 'Each spoke in her own language; neither understood the other's words; both were very watchful, and intent to deduce from look and manner, what the unintelligible words meant.' Miss Pross dismisses her opponent's language as 'nonsensical.' Yet they communicate non-verbally, one motivated by the 'vigorous tenacity of love,' the other by sheer hatred. As with Darnay and his mother, and Carton and the young girl at the end of the novel, the eyes are the key to this nonrational language:

> 'It will do her no good to keep herself concealed from me at this moment,' said Madame Defarge. 'Good patriots will know what that means. Let me see her. Go tell her that I wish to see her. Do you hear?'

> 'If those eyes of yours were bed-winches,' returned Miss Pross, 'and I was an English four-poster, they shouldn't loose a splinter of me. No, you wicked foreign woman; I am your match.'

Madame Defarge's attack is a parodic version of Sydney Carton's self-sacrifice in the next chapter: 'if she had been ordered to the axe tomorrow,' her only response would have been 'a fierce desire to change places with the man who sent her there'; rendered 'lifeless' by a pistol shot, she symbolically re-enters the unseen world when Pross locks her body in and throws the key into the same river Carton has already mentally followed to death.

—Tom Lloyd, "Language, Love and Identity: *A Tale of Two Cities*," *Dickensian* 88, no. 3 (Autumn 1992): pp. 158–160.

Works by
Charles Dickens

Sketches by "Boz," Illustrative of Every-day Life and Every-day People. 1836. 2 vols.

Sunday under Three Heads. 1836.

The Village Coquettes: A Comic Opera. 1836.

The Posthumous Papers of the Pickwick Club. 1836–37. 20 parts.

The Strange Gentleman: A Comic Burletta. 1837.

Memoirs of Joseph Grimaldi (editor). 1838. 2 vols.

Sketches of Young Gentlemen. 1838.

Oliver Twist; or, The Parish Boy's Progress. 1838. 3 vols.

The Life and Adventures of Nicholas Nickleby. 1838–39. 20 parts.

The Loving Ballad of Lord Bateman (with William Makepeace Thackeray). 1839.

Sketches of Young Couples. 1840.

Master Humphrey's Clock; The Old Curiosity Shop; Barnaby Rudge. 1840–41. 88 parts.

The Pic Nic Papers (editor). 1841. 3 vols.

American Notes. 1842. 2 vols.

A Christmas Carol in Prose: Being a Ghost-Story of Christmas. 1843.

The Life and Adventures of Martin Chuzzlewit, His Relatives, Friends and Enemies. 1843–44. 20 parts.

The Chimes: A Goblin Story of Some Bells That Rang an Old Year Out and a New Year In. 1845.

The Cricket on the Hearth: A Fairy Tale of Home. 1846.

Pictures from Italy. 1846.

The Battle of Life: A Love Story. 1846.

Dealings with the Firm of Dombey and Son Wholesale, Retail and for Exportation. 1846–48. 20 parts.

An Appeal to Fallen Women. 1847.

Works. 1847–67. 17 vols.

The Haunted Man and the Ghost's Bargain: A Fancy for Christmas Time. 1848.

Elegy Written in a Country Churchyard. c. 1849.

The Personal History, Adventures, Experiences and Observations of David Copperfield the Younger. 1849–50. 20 parts.

Mr. Nightingale's Diary: A Farce (with Mark Lemon). 1851.

Bleak House. 1852–53. 20 parts.

A Child's History of England. 1852–54. 3 vols.

Hard Times, for These Times. 1854.

Speech Delivered at the Meeting of the Administrative Reform Association. 1855.

Little Dorrit. 1855–57. 20 parts.

Novels and Tales Reprinted from Household Words (editor). 1856–59. 11 vols.

The Case of the Reformers in the Literary Fund (with others). 1858.

Speech at the Anniversary Festival of the Hospital for Sick Children. 1858.

Speech at the First Festival Dinner of the Playground and Recreation Society. 1858.

Works (Library Edition). 1858–59 (22 vols.), 1861–74 (30 vols.).

A Tale of Two Cities. 1859. 8 parts.

Christmas Stories from Household Words. 1859. 9 parts.

Great Expectations. 1861. 3 vols.

Great Expectations: A Drama. 1861.

The Uncommercial Traveller. 1861.

An Address on Behalf of the Printer's Pension Society. c. 1864.

Speech at the North London or University College Hospital: Anniversary Dinner in Aid of the Funds. 1864.

Our Mutual Friend. 1864–65. 20 parts.

The Frozen Deep (with Wilkie Collins). 1866.

No Thoroughfare (with Wilkie Collins). 1867.

Speech at the Railway Benevolent Institution: Ninth Annual Dinner. 1867.

Works (Charles Dickens Edition). 1867–75. 21 vols.

Christmas Stories from All the Year Round. c. 1868. 9 parts.

The Readings of Mr. Charles Dickens, as Condensed by Himself. 1868.

Address Delivered at the Birmingham and Midland Institute. 1869.

A Curious Dance round a Curious Tree (with W. H. Wills). 1870.

Speech at Chairman of the Anniversary Festival Dinner of the Royal Free Hospital. 1870.

The Mystery of Edwin Drood. 1870. 6 parts.

Speeches Literary and Social. Ed. R. H. Shepherd. 1870.

The Newsvendors' Benevolent and Provident Institution: Speeches in Behalf of the Institution. 1871.

Is She His Wife? or Something Singular: A Comic Burletta. c. 1872.

The Lamplighter: A Farce. 1879.

The Mudfog Papers, etc. 1880.

Letters. Ed. Georgina Hogarth and Mary Dickens. 1880–1882. 3 vols.

Plays and Poems, with a Few Miscellanies in Prose Now First Collected. Ed. R. H. Shepherd. 1885. 2 vols.

The Lazy Tour of Two Idle Apprentices; No Thoroughfare; The Perils of Certain English Prisoners (with Wilkie Collins). 1890.

Works (Macmillan Edition). 1892–1925. 21 vols.

Letters to Wilkie Collins 1851–1870. Ed. Lawrence Hutton. 1892.

Works (Gadshill Edition). Ed. Andrew Lang. 1897–1908. 36 vols.

To Be Read at Dusk and Other Stories, Sketches and Essays. Ed. F. G. Kitton. 1898.

Christmas Stories from Household Words and All the Year Round. 1898. 5 vols.

Works (Biographical Edition). Ed. Arthur Waugh. 1902–03. 19 vols.

Poems and Verses. Ed. F. G. Kitton. 1903.

Works (National Edition). Ed. Bertram W. Matz. 1906–08. 40 vols.

Dickens and Maria Beadnell: Private Correspondence. Ed. G. P. Baker. 1908.

The Dickens-Kolle Letters. Ed. Harry B. Smith. 1910.

Works (Centenary Edition). 1910–11. 36 vols.

Dickens as Editor: Letters Written by Him to William Henry Wills, His Sub-Editor. Ed. R. C. Lehmann. 1912.

Works (Waverley Edition). 1913–18. 30 vols.

Unpublished Letters to Mark Lemon. Ed. Walter Dexter. 1927.

Letters to the Baroness Burdett-Coutts. Ed. Charles C. Osborne. 1931.

Dickens to His Oldest Friend: The Letters of a Lifetime to Thomas Beard. Ed. Walter Dexter. 1932.

Letters to Charles Lever. Ed. Flora V. Livingston. 1933.

Mr. and Mrs. Charles Dickens: His Letters to Her. Ed. Walter Dexter. 1935.

The Love Romance of Dickens, Told in His Letters to Maria Beadnell (Mrs. Winter). Ed. Walter Dexter. 1936.

The Nonesuch Dickens. Ed. Arthur Waugh, Hugh Walpole, Walter Dexter, and Thomas Hatton. 1937–38. 23 vols.

Letters. Ed. Walter Dexter. 1938. 3 vols.

The New Oxford Illustrated Dickens. 1947–58. 21 vols.

Speeches. Ed. K. J. Fielding, 1960, 1988.

Letters (Pilgrim Edition). Ed. Madeline House, Graham Storey, Kathleen Tillotson et al. 1965– .

The Clarendon Dickens. Ed. John Butt, Kathleen Tillotson, and James Kinsley. 1966– .

Uncollected Writings from Household Words 1850–1859. Ed. Harry Stone. 1968.

Complete Plays and Selected Poems. 1970.

Dickens in Europe: Essays. Ed. Rosalind Vallance. 1975.

The Public Readings. Ed. Phillip Collins. 1975.

Supernatural Short Stories. Ed. Michael Hayes. 1978.

The Annotated Dickens. Ed. Edward Giuliano and Philip Collins. 1986. 2 vols.

Dickens' Working Notes for His Novels. Ed. Harry Stone. 1987.

Sketches by Boz and Other Early Papers 1833–39. Ed. Michael Slater. 1994.

Works about
Charles Dickens

Ackroyd, Peter. *Dickens*. New York: Harper Collins, 1990.

Barnard, Robert. *Imagery and Theme in the Novels of Dickens*. Oslo: Universitetsforlaget, 1974.

Bloom, Harold, ed. *Charles Dickens*. New York: Chelsea House, 1987.

Brook, George L. *The Language of Dickens*. London: Andre Deutsch, 1970.

Butt, John, and Kathleen Tillotson. *Dickens at Work*. London: Chatto & Windus, 1958.

Carey, John. *The Violent Effigy: A Study of Dickens' Imagination*. London: Faber & Faber, 1973.

Carlisle, Janice. *The Sense of an Audience: Dickens, Thackeray, and George Eliot at Mid-Century*. Athens: University of Georgia Press, 1981.

Cockshut, A. O. J. *The Imagination of Charles Dickens*. New York: New York University Press, 1962.

Daldry, Graham. *Charles Dickens and the Form of the Novel*. Totowa, NJ: Barnes & Noble, 1987.

Dyson, A. E. *The Inimitable Dickens: A Reading of the Novels*. London: Macmillan, 1970.

Fielding, K. J. *Charles Dickens: A Critical Introduction*. London: Longmans, Green, 1958.

Frank, Lawrence. *Charles Dickens and the Romantic Self*. Lincoln: University of Nebraska Press, 1984.

Gilbert, Elliot L. " 'To Awake from History': Carlyle, Thackeray, and *A Tale of Two Cities*." *Dickens Studies Annual* 12 (1983): pp. 247-65.

Gold, Joseph. *Charles Dickens: Radical Moralist*. Minneapolis: University of Minnesota Press, 1972.

Goldberg, Michael. *Carlyle and Dickens*. Athens: University of Georgia Press, 1972.

Guerard, Albert J. *The Triumph of the Novel: Dickens, Dostoevsky, Faulkner*. New York: Oxford University Press, 1976.

Hardy, Barbara. *The Moral Art of Dickens*. New York: Oxford University Press, 1970.

Herst, Beth R. *The Dickens Hero: Selfhood and Alienation in the Dickens World*. New York: AMS Press, 1990.

Holbrook, David. *Charles Dickens and the Image of Woman*. New York: New York University Press, 1993.

Hornback, Bert G. *"Noah's Arkitecture": A Study of Dickens's Mythology*. Athens: Ohio University Press, 1972.

Houston, Gail Turley. *Consuming Fictions; Gender, Class, and Hunger in Dickens's Novels*. Carbondale: Southern Illinois University Press, 1994.

Ingham, Patricia. *Dickens, Women, and Language*. Toronto: University of Toronto Press, 1992.

Johnson, Edgar H. *Charles Dickens: His Tragedy and Triumph*. Rev. ed. London: Allen Lane, 1977.

Kincaid, James R. *Dickens and the Rhetoric of Laughter*. Oxford: Clarendon Press, 1971.

Kucich, John. *Excess and Restraint in the Novels of Charles Dickens*. Athens: University of Georgia Press, 1981.

Leavis, F. R., and Q. D. Leavis. *Dickens the Novelist*. London: Chatto & Windus, 1970.

Lettis, Richard. *The Dickens Aesthetic*. New York: AMS Press, 1989.

Lucas, John. *The Melancholy Man: A Study of Dickens's Novels*. Totowa, NJ: Barnes & Noble, 1980.

Manning, Sylvia Bank. *Dickens as Satirist*. New Haven: Yale University Press, 1971.

Miller, J. Hillis. *Charles Dickens: The World of His Novels*. Cambridge, MA: Harvard University Press, 1958.

Miyoshi, Masao. *The Divided Self: A Perspective on the Literature of the Victorians*. New York: New York University Press, 1969.

Monod, Sylvère. *Dickens the Novelist*. Norman: University of Oklahoma Press, 1968.

Morgan, Nicholas H. *Secret Journeys: Theory and Practice in Reading Dickens*. Rutherford, NJ: Fairleigh Dickinson University Press, 1992.

Nelson, Harland S. *Charles Dickens*. Boston: Twayne, 1981.

Newcomb, Mildred. *The Imagined World of Charles Dickens*. Columbus: Ohio State University Press, 1989.

Nisber, Ada, and Blake Nevius, eds. *Dickens Centennial Essays*. Berkeley: University of California Press, 1971.

Page, Norman. *A Dickens Companion*. London: Macmillan, 1984.

Praz, Mario. "Charles Dickens." In Praz's *The Hero in Eclipse in Victorian*

Fiction. Tr. Angus Davidson. London: Oxford University Press, 1956, pp. 127-88.

Raina, Badri. *Dickens and the Dialectic of Growth*. Madison: University of Wisconsin Press, 1986.

Schad, John. *The Reader in the Dickensian Mirror: Some New Language*. New York: St. Martin's Press, 1992.

Schwarzbach, F. W. *Dickens and the City*. London: Athione Press, 1979.

Slater, Michael, ed. *Dickens 1970: Centenary Essays*. London: Chapman & Hall, 1970.

Solomon, Pearl Chesler. *Dickens and Melville in Their Time*. New York: Columbia University Press, 1975.

Spence, Gordon. "Dickens as a Historical Novelist." *Dickensian* 72 (1976): pp. 21–30.

Stewart, Garrett. *Dickens and the Trials of Imagination*. Cambridge, MA: Harvard University Press, 1974.

Stoehr, Taylor. *Dickens: The Dreamer's Stance*. Ithaca, NY: Cornell University Press, 1965.

Stone, Harry. *Dickens and the Invisible World: Fairy Tales, Fantasy, and Novel-Making*. Bloomington: Indiana University Press, 1979.

———. *The Night Side of Dickens: Cannibalism, Passion, Necessity*. Columbus: Ohio State University Press, 1994.

Sucksmith, Harvey Peter. *The Narrative Art of Charles Dickens*. Oxford: Clarendon Press, 1970.

Thurley, Geoffrey. *The Dickens Myth: Its Genesis and Structure*. London: Routledge & Kegan Paul, 1976.

Vogel, Jane. *Allegory in Dickens*. Mobile: University of Alabama Press, 1977.

Welsh, Alexander. *The City of Dickens*. Oxford: Clarendon Press, 1971.

———. *From Copyright to Copperfield: The Identity of Dickens*. Cambridge, MA: Harvard University Press, 1987.

Williams, Raymond. *The English Novel: From Dickens to Lawrence*. London: Chatto & Windus, 1970.

Index of
Themes and Ideas